Testing
The Fire

Mark D. J. Smith

First published in Great Britain in 1996
by St Matthew Publishing Ltd
Copyright © Mark D.J. Smith

ISBN 0 9524672 7 5

St Matthew Publishing Ltd
24 Geldart St
Cambridge CB1 2LX UK
Tel: +44 (0)1223 363545, Fax +44 (0)1223 512304

Email: aak66@dial.pipex.com
http:www.phar.cam.ac.uk/StMatts/

Printed in Great Britain

Contents

CONTENTS

Historical Note

In early 1996 the church at the centre of the 'Toronto Blessing' left the Vineyard group of churches and changed its name from Toronto Airport Vineyard to Toronto Airport Fellowship. In this book I have generally used the former name, but have used the latter when referring to it in the present or future.

Mark Smith

Foreword

The charismatic renewal has never lacked for either enthusiastic promoters or implacable opponents, but it has often looked in vain for careful discerners of what is and what is not of God in its teaching and practice. Revivalist movements tend by their very nature to encourage one hundred per cent acceptance of their authenticity among their supporters and to discountenance those whose verdict is of the "Yes, but..." kind, who want to temper an overall grateful acceptance with questions and corrections of different kinds.

We need to remember that among the gifts of the Spirit listed in 1 Corinthians 12 is that of spiritual discernment and that John in his first letter enjoins us to test the spirits. This book is such an exercise in discernment and is concerned particularly with that phase of the renewal that has come to be known as the 'Toronto blessing'. The first fine careless rapture is over, some of the fruits are being gathered and it is more than timely to expose the whole matter to a sympathetic scrutiny by someone who acknowledges both the authority of scripture and the renewing action of the Spirit in the Church, but who wants to make sure that delight in dramatic manifestations and personal renewals does not distract us from asking the searching questions which will allow the truth to emerge.

That is the task that Mark Smith has with considerable thoroughness undertaken in this book and it is important that his conclusions be taken seriously by all who have been involved in "Toronto" as well as by its critics. He writes out of personal contact with the movement, but, more importantly, out of a deep concern for the scriptural gospel and that it should be proclaimed and responded to in a balanced way in today's church.

I commend his work and the questions he raises to those who read the book. If at some points the questioner himself needs to be questioned, that is all part of the task of discernment in which it is of prime importance that we should all be continually involved, so that what God is saying by his Spirit and in his Word may be more clearly heard.

Tom Smail

Preface

In the year since I completed the manuscript of this book a number of things have changed. The 'fire' which originally characterised the 'Toronto Blessing' seems to have receded somewhat, in Britain at least. In some ways, church life has returned to normal. Churches which two years ago were being shaken to their foundations have become more settled, content perhaps to allow the embers of the 'Toronto Blessing' to smoulder gently. But smouldering embers can quickly flare up again, and so I believe the issues discussed in this book are still relevant.

In particular, it is vitally important that churches begin to think carefully through the question of what it means to be 'biblical'. In what follows I argue that such thinking was woefully lacking in the early days of the 'Toronto Blessing', and offer my own view of where a careful weighing of the movement in the light of the Bible ought to lead. I hope that what I say will at least contribute to serious debate on these matters. If such a debate does not take place, the suspicion will be very strong that, despite claims to the contrary, the Bible has no important place in a large number of so-called 'Bible-believing' churches.

Numerous factors have contributed to my writing this book. I am grateful to many people for many things. But during the last two turbulent years, when loyalties to church, friends and beliefs have been set in great tension, a few people in particular have helped enormously. First is Rachel, who—and this is perhaps the least of her contributions—has trusted my judgement despite great pressures to the contrary.

Second, Gregor has been a great friend. The knowledge that I was not struggling alone has been a source of strength; and our conversations in pubs—where Steve also had a considerable part to play—on putting greens and over the 'phone were a great help. Third, Peter has been a friend but at the same time a church leader with enough faith to accept and even welcome my difficult questions. Thanks to Mum and Dad, who might not understand (though there again they might!) quite why Christian things are so important to me, but have never failed in love and friendship. Finally, thanks to Philip, David and Glenn at St Matthew Publishing for their hard work in turning a tatty manuscript into this book.

Mark Smith

Testing The Fire

A Biblical Analysis of the 'Blessing'

Introduction

1994-95 was an extraordinary time for British Christians. They encountered something seemingly never seen before, a strange new form of church life that impacted almost every stream of Christianity in Britain. It touched some Christians and their churches only slightly, but many others it turned upside down. It has come to be known, rightly or wrongly, as the 'Toronto Blessing'.

In August of 1994, the 'Toronto Blessing' came to my church. I found myself in a Sunday service at which one man started jumping vigorously up and down, shaking violently all the time, for about half an hour, until he was bright red and soaked with sweat. He was 'pogo-ing in the Spirit'. Some people began to fall over backwards. Others trembled, laughed, cried, shouted, boxed the air. Still others had their torsos jerked violently at random moments. One man was unable to speak; another stood absolutely still, half bent over in a strangely contorted position. This was repeated in later Sunday services. Extra meetings were arranged so that we could 'receive' more.

The people involved were not strangers to me. They were close and less close friends, and respected leaders. And they were testifying to the wonder of their experiences, to the marvellous things God was doing in them. I felt intense pressure to get involved. So, deciding to allow the possibility that this might be God, one Sunday service in early September I stood, along with a number of others, with my hands outstretched and eyes closed, and waited to be prayed for. I did not actively want something to happen, but I said to God that it was his right to do something if he wanted and here I was, ready.

Nothing happened. In a way this was a disappointment, because I had thought that if something happened all my questions would be resolved. If I experienced what everyone was talking about I would be able—despite the questions—to conclude that God had done something tangible in me. I suppose I hoped that if something happened that was not my own doing, then I would be able to believe the 'Toronto Blessing' truly was from God. Unfortunately, the fact that nothing happened did not enable me to conclude the opposite. Just because God had not blessed me did not mean he was not blessing others. So I continued attending meetings, observing what was going on and thinking about its implications.

I was in turmoil. I had immense doubts that the things I saw could really be from God. Yet many, many people, including respected leaders and close friends, were declaring it indeed was from God. I felt excluded. I attended worship services which focused almost entirely on the 'Blessing'—on something I did not believe in and could not feel part of. Worship became an impossibility for me in such services. I tried to rejoice with those who had been 'Blessed', yet I could not help but suspect that in the long run their experience would turn bad.

None of this is unique. There are large numbers of Christians who have felt as I did. Some of them have pressed on, standing up to be prayed for and eventually receiving a 'blessing'. Others have adjusted to the situation, accepting that the 'Blessing' is not for them, but remaining quietly in their church. Others, like myself, have felt the need to register their disquiet with their leaders, and have even felt the need to move to another church where they can worship happily.

In this book I have set out my understanding of the 'Toronto Blessing', hoping it will help other Christians who have similar doubts to come to terms with them and to find a way forward at this difficult time. I have also written it in the hope that it will explain to those who are sure the 'Blessing' is from God, why people like myself cannot accept their assurances. Finally, I have written it in an attempt to be faithful to God's Word to us in and through the Bible.

Précis

It is worth setting out in brief the route I follow in the book. This will enable the reader to know exactly where he or she is in the argument, and so to understand why I reach the conclusions I do.

Chapter 1 explains why it is important—whatever our point of view about the particular issue of the 'Toronto Blessing'—that all Christians be open to criticism.

Chapters 2 to 4 offer an analysis and criticism of the attempts that have been made to demonstrate that the 'Blessing' and the results it produces are biblical.

Chapters 5 and 6 examine the particular types of thinking and practice which have enabled the strange experiences of the 'Toronto Blessing' to be accepted so readily by so many Christians.

Chapters 7 and 8 explain what I think the strange experiences associated with the 'Blessing' really are.

Chapter 9 and Conclusion offer a biblical perspective on the issues raised by the 'Blessing'.

Two Appendices address some further issues raised during the main argument of the book.

A Word about Explanations

Some people who read this book will suspect it is an attempt to do away with the miraculous and to explain away mysteries. If they use technical language, they will say they suspect the book of 'reductionism'. Behind the suspicion there lies a fear. It is a fear held by many modern believers: that explanations erode the need for faith and finally erode the need for God. After all, did not Darwin's explanation of the origin of the species erode people's belief in a Creator? Do not modern science's explanations erode belief in miracles? Thus will not explanation of the 'Toronto Blessing' phenomena erode faith in a God who acts today?

Behind this fear there in turn lies a misunderstanding. It is the misunderstanding which thinks that the modern world is a place without belief. It is the misunderstanding which thinks that any belief is better than no belief. It is the misunderstanding which leads to the fear that people who explain things are on the side of unbelief and will eventually explain God away.

But the modern world is not a place without belief. There are more believers, more religions and pseudo-religions, more cults, more secular faiths and alternative spiritualities, now than ever before. A recent poll found that 97 per cent of Americans believe in God. For many, it is not the Judaeo-Christian God, 'but "higher consciousness"—with extra-sensory perception and communication with the dead thrown in for good measure'.[1] Nor is the modern world without a sense of mystery. There are more 'signs', 'wonders' and 'miracles' going on in the name of different religions and different gurus than could possibly be counted. From tear-stained statues of Mary to milk-drinking Hindu idols, we are surrounded by the 'miraculous'. From herbal potions and positive-thinking to crystal pyramids, we can choose any wonder-cure we wish.

As Christians we need to realise that what is at stake is *not belief, but belief in the Living God*. To put it another way, the issue is not between belief and unbelief, but between true and false belief, between belief which leads to life and belief which leads to death. We need to realise that faith in the living God is not the same as faith in the seemingly miraculous. To be sure, faith in the Living God is faith in the God who does miracles, but it is not faith in anything that seems 'strange' or 'wonderful'.

That might seem obvious enough when strange things occur in the name of other religions. However, it also true when strange things happen in the name of Christianity. Christianity is not immune to error. Christians, like everybody else, are capable of putting their faith in the wrong place. Therefore, it is vital that we be open to the possibility that the strange things in our midst can be explained.

We live in an age of Transcendental Meditation, 'soul retrieval' techniques, astrologers, UFOs, New Agers and wonder-working gurus. If, in the midst of all this, we wish our witness to be truly distinctive, Christians must be more discerning, not less. If our faith really is faith in the Living God, then it will be faith which is determined to question the source of all things and reject that which does not come from him, so that he can be glorified all the more for that which does.

The 'Toronto Blessing' is undoubtedly a 'strange thing'. It is, as many say, 'a sign causing people to wonder'. Nevertheless, we must be prepared to ask the questions, what is it a sign of and what are we wondering about?

NOTES
1. Reported in *Third Way* magazine (September 1995, vol. 18.7), p. 12.

CHAPTER 1

Asking Questions

This book has two main parts. In the first part, Chapters 2 to 4, I will explain how those involved in the 'Toronto Blessing' have sought to relate the Bible to what they have experienced. I will seek to show how, in many ways, their attempts have been unsatisfactory. Then, from Chapter 5 onwards, I will offer what I think is a more satisfactory biblical approach to the 'Blessing'. At regular points I will be criticising the views of other Christians. Consequently, I need to begin by dealing with the commonly-held belief that we should not criticise each other.

Criticising Each Other

The idea that Christians should be wary of being critical is a common one. There are a number of factors involved, some right and some wrong, and it is worth separating them out so that I can explain in what sense criticism is right and necessary.

First, it is true that as a general principle Christians should be positive rather than negative, seeking to speak good of one another whenever possible. We are people for whom and in whom God has done wonderful things, and our attitudes and behaviour should reflect this. Paul says of personal relationships, 'Let love be genuine; hate what is evil, hold fast to what is good; love one another with brotherly affection; outdo one another in showing honour' (Rom 12.9-10).

We should always seek to think the best we can of each other. When we see others doing or saying things we disagree with, we should not rush to criticise. We should be sure that what we dislike is not trivial or insignificant. We should consider whether what we have to say will do good, or is merely criticism for its own sake. We should give those with whom we disagree the benefit of the doubt with respect to their motives, assuming they are seeking to serve God in what they are doing unless there is clear evidence to the contrary. At the same time, we should be vigilant as to our own motives.

However, if we have something to say that will do good or keep others from harm, then it is our duty to speak out. The fact that God has done great things for us and in us does not mean nothing can go wrong in the body of Christ. If we allow a desire to 'be positive' to blind us to that, then we are failing the church. Paul, James, Peter and John were all aware of wrong in the churches of New Testament times, and they were not afraid to analyse and judge those errors. At times, their criticisms had an extremely strong tone, as, for instance, Paul's letter to the Galatians.

The mention of criticism does raise two important questions, though. First, were not Paul, James, Peter and John all apostles, giving them a right to criticise that we do not have? Second, did they not put their criticisms personally and directly to the churches with which they had difficulties? We can generalise these questions by saying the first is about position, while the second is about method. Do we have to be put in certain positions by God before we have the right to criticise? And should our criticisms be delivered only in a certain way?

Position to Criticise?

The first thing to be said on this issue is that when God puts people in positions he does give them the right to criticise. As apostles and leaders of churches, Paul, James, Peter and John all had the right to tell their churches where they were going wrong and to direct them as to what they should do. Leaders of churches today certainly have similar rights in their own churches.

Does this mean that nobody else has the right to criticise? I believe not. Actually, 'the right to criticise' is probably not the best phrase. In Old Testament times, when Israel went wrong God raised up prophets whose *duty* it was to criticise. It seems very likely to me that Israel's leaders would often have objected that such prophets had no 'right to criticise'. But because of their sense of duty, of obedience to God, the prophets continued to speak out. The church era has not been much different. Christians have tended not to designate people like Martin Luther as 'prophets', but such people have fulfilled the same function. Luther saw terrible abuses in the church, and he believed it was his duty to speak out against them. People objected that he was a mere monk, with no right to criticise the Pope and cardinals. But Luther knew his duty was to God, not to man.

There are surely times when people who do not have 'the right' to criticise by virtue of 'position' do have 'the right' by virtue of 'duty'. At such times speaking out becomes a matter for the individual conscience before God—those who do so must seek to be obedient to God's will.

In addition, there is another 'position' for criticism which we have not yet considered. Namely the position of ordinary Christians, who are called by God to constructively seek, in partnership with their fellow believers, the best form of Christianity for their present situation. Although God puts put some believers in leadership over others, it remains that we are all equal. We are part of the priesthood of all believers (see 1 Pet. 2.9), and as such we each have the right and duty to contribute to seeking the way forward.

Participation in this task will involve us thinking about what we do and how we do it, what we believe and why. Ideally, all Christians would contribute to this process, although it is often left to those who are more theologically minded. However, within this process, it would be naïve to think that only positive things will ever need to be said. No Christian will ever make a perfect contribution. There will always be parts of what is said that are good and deserve to be taken on board, and other parts that should be rejected. If the process is operating well, then no Christian will mind having the bad parts of their contribution criticised. They will instead be glad of the privilege of being part of the search for what the nature of today's church should be. It is my belief that if this process were operating properly it would provide a good deal of room for 'criticism' in the church. Naturally, this would not be destructive criticism of people, but constructive criticism of ideas and methods.

Methods of Criticism

Let us move on to the question of *how* criticism should be delivered. Should it only ever be in the form of personal, direct communication? The answer follows from what has already been said about the 'positions' from which we criticise.

For leaders engaged in criticising churches and Christians over whom they have authority, it is obviously best to bring their comments in the form of direct, personal communication. It would be wrong to communicate such matters to anybody else. Direct, personal communication is entirely appropriate in that case, but is it appropriate in others?

One common idea is that with other types of criticism we should follow the model of Matthew 18. That is, we should first take our complaint in person to the one whom we think has done wrong. Only if he or she refuses to listen should we make the complaint public. But Mt. 18.15-17 refers to a situation in which a person feels he or she has been sinned against by another member of his or her local fellowship. The passage sets out the procedure to be followed in this particular circumstance. If, for example, I felt someone was spreading lies about me within my fellowship, I would follow the Matthew 18 procedure. However, it does not follow that when I perceive a leader to be teaching false doctrine in another church I should automatically refer to Matthew 18. The leader has not sinned against me personally. Yet it may be that the false doctrine is damaging people and bringing God's name into disrepute, in which case I may consider it my duty to speak out. In this and many other cases Matthew 18 does not apply.

Or, it could be that a person is not seeking to bring criticism in that sense at all. It may simply be that he or she wants to contribute to the process I outlined earlier in which all of us as the priesthood of true believers have the right to participate. Matthew 18.15-17 is not relevant to this situation either. People are not being denounced, accused of sin, or anything like that. Rather, ideas, theology and ways of doing things are being constructively criticised.

Practically speaking, when criticism is brought in this spirit Christians are at liberty to make their contribution in whatever form they deem appropriate. At local church level this is most likely to take the form of participation in discussion groups, verbal and written suggestions to leaders, circulated papers, and so on. On a wider level, it might take the form of contributions to theological journals, Christian magazines, and published books and pamphlets. As long as everything is done in a Christian spirit, there is no reason why we should not say critical things in these forms.

Finally, what of those who are fulfilling a more 'prophetic' role in their criticism? How should they make themselves heard? We need to remember that prophets often have to bring unpopular messages. Their criticisms can be unwelcome, perhaps especially to those in leadership positions, and so Christians are inclined to block their ears. I believe it follows from this that they should make themselves heard *in whatever way they can*. I see no justification at all for barring them from making public statements in whatever form is appropriate. Certainly the prophets of the Old Testament made use of all kinds of strange public methods in order to get the people's attention!

Criticising God

There is one category of criticism I have not dealt with so far. It is a kind of criticism which supporters of the 'Toronto Blessing' have regularly warned their 'opponents' against. It would be better, they say, to keep quiet than to criticise the 'Blessing' and find yourself criticising what God is doing. This has become known as the 'Gamaliel Principle', because it is the reasoning the Pharisee Gamaliel followed in Acts 5. In some cases this principle is combined with warnings against 'calling good things evil'. Mark Stibbe, a leading charismatic theologian, takes this line, even arguing that those who criticise the 'Toronto Blessing' 'need to be very careful not to commit the unforgivable sin—namely, blaspheming against the Holy Spirit.'[1] I will consider this serious charge first, and then look at the 'Gamaliel Principle'.

Blasphemy

What can we say of the very serious charge that criticism of the 'Toronto Blessing' amounts to blasphemy against the Holy Spirit? If my own experience is anything to go by, critics will have spent long hours pondering the question of whether the 'Blessing' is of God. They will have considered the gravity of the possibility that they are criticising a work of God. They will also have spent time considering the consequences of that possibility. I know I have. Over a prolonged period of time I watched the 'Blessing' come into and take over the life of my church. I attended meetings, listened to what friends and leaders had to say, and read every publication about the matter available to me.

Throughout, I had grave doubts about the 'Blessing'. I eventually concluded that it was not, as far as I could see, what its supporters claimed. This book goes some way to explaining why I reached this conclusion. My point here, however, is that I knew my conclusion meant I would have to make known my criticisms. Therefore I had to take seriously the possibility that I might be publicly criticising a work of God. I knew it was not impossible that I could be wrong. However, I also knew that, as far as I could see, I was not wrong, and it was my responsibility before God to do what I believed to be right.

I suppose that is why it did not occur to me that my criticisms of the 'Toronto Blessing' might be blasphemy against the Holy Spirit: the unforgivable sin. Perhaps I should have considered the possibility. Mark Stibbe's warning is very serious. I hope it is not the intention, but his and others' warnings of a similar kind often sound like scare tactics. I will assume they are not just attempts to apply a 'spiritual strong-arm', and that those who utter them are earnest about what they say. As Mark Stibbe has offered the fullest version of the argument, in what follows I will respond in detail to his views.

First of all, we need to ascertain what exactly Stibbe thinks 'blasphemy against the Holy Spirit' is. Initially it seems clear. On the basis of Mk 3.29 and Mt. 12.32 he defines it as 'calling the works of the Holy Spirit demonic'. Although I am critical of the 'Toronto Blessing', I do not think that either the strange physical manifestations or the so-called 'fruit' are demonic in character or origin. This then seems to remove myself, and others who take a similar line, from the danger of 'blaspheming'. Unfortunately, Stibbe then broadens things out. Those in danger of 'blaspheming' are not just people who call the 'Blessing' demonic, but, 'those who are opposed to the Toronto blessing'—they 'are hostile and resistant when it comes to the current work of the Holy Spirit'.[2]

This seems to imply that *any* criticism of the 'Blessing' is blasphemy against the Holy Spirit, not just that which calls it demonic. This must be what Stibbe means, because he concludes by offering only one option for critics other than blasphemy: to keep quiet. He characterises (in a very sweeping and doubtful manner) people who oppose the 'Blessing' as, 'those of a conservative evangelical or of an institutional mind-set', and says they,

> need to be very careful not to blaspheme against
> the Holy Spirit ... when they speak about the Toronto
> blessing. A much more Godly response would be that
> of Gamaliel in Acts 5:38... If you are a sceptic, I
> respectfully counsel you to take this line.[3]

We consider the 'Gamaliel Principle' later. Suffice to say that it seems remarkable to describe Gamaliel's advice not to put some Christians to death as 'Godly'. It may be 'worldly-wise', but it hardly qualifies as being, 'Godly'. Indeed, although the apostles were set free, they were still beaten and charged not to speak in the name of Jesus (Acts 5.40)!

That aside, my point is that in offering silence as the only alternative to blasphemy against the Holy Spirit, Stibbe's argument characterises *all* serious criticism of the 'Toronto Blessing' as blasphemous, not merely that criticism which concludes that it is demonic. We need to look at the biblical texts to see if this idea can be sustained.

The key verses are:

> *I tell you, every sin and blasphemy will be forgiven men, but the blasphemy against the Spirit will not be forgiven. And whoever says a word against the Son of man will be forgiven; but whoever speaks against the Holy Spirit will not be forgiven, either in this age or in the age to come.*   (Mt. 12.31-32)

> *Truly, I say to you, all sins will be forgiven the sons of men, and whatever blasphemies they utter; but whoever blasphemes against the Holy Spirit never has forgiveness, but is guilty of an eternal sin.*   (Mk 3.28-29)

Both of these sayings come in the context of controversy with the Jewish authorities. They have accused Jesus of being able to cast demons out of people only because 'the prince of demons' is in him. Jesus defends himself with the retort that it is ridiculous to think this since it would mean Satan is divided against himself. As Stibbe rightly says, 'The issue is whether Jesus is performing extraordinary deeds by the power of the Holy Spirit or by the power of Satan.'[4]

This is the context which helps us begin to understand what 'blasphemy against the Holy Spirit' is. It can indeed be defined as Stibbe defines it: 'calling the works of the Holy Spirit demonic'.[5] However this is just where the problems begin. The dilemma is how it can be, if Jesus' death on the cross brought forgiveness for all sins, that there is nevertheless one sin which remains unforgivable. It has long been recognised that the question of how we should apply 'the unforgivable sin' to Christian life is extremely difficult to answer. Young Christians especially read these verses and wonder if, unknowingly, they have committed this sin and whether, as a result, they will not be saved after all. This is an example of the tremendous difficulty the church has had in knowing how to apply the sayings about blasphemy against the Holy Spirit.

That does not mean we should run away from the texts or ignore them. The Bible *is* difficult to understand in places, but we should always attempt to do so and apply its teachings appropriately. However, the difficulty the church has had in the past with 'the unforgivable sin' indicates that we should treat it with considerable caution. Christians too quickly use it as a stick to bash their fellow-believers with.

I am assuming, of course, that it is still possible for critics of the 'Blessing' to be 'fellow-believers'. If it is accepted that they are indeed Christians, then the often-made equation (found for example in Stibbe's book) of critics with the 'teachers of the law' and the 'Pharisees' who implacably opposed Jesus, seems very unfair. This equation highlights the error of the 'blasphemy' accusation in the current situation. There is no real parallel between these 'Pharisees' and 'teachers of the law' and critics of the 'Blessing' such as myself. Those who make the equation are playing on the common practice of using the example of the Pharisees to warn Christians against developing self-righteous, bigoted 'religious' attitudes. Stibbe says,

> There are a number of people in the church, who correspond to Mark's 'teachers of the law' and Matthew's 'Pharisees'. They are very religious people. Some of them love the church (perhaps a little more than they should). Some of them read the Word and are wholeheartedly committed to Bible study and teaching. But in spite of these dutiful qualities, they are hostile and resistant when it comes to the current work of the Holy Spirit.[6]

One wonders whether this is a picture derived from personal acquaintance with critics, or perhaps a pre-conceived caricature derived for polemic needs. My own experience is that critics of the 'Blessing' are of many different 'types'.

Be that as it may, the important thing to notice is the characterization of critics as 'very religious'. What 'very religious' means Stibbe does not specify. Rather, he makes use of the strong association in Christians' minds between the terms 'religious' and 'Pharisees'. Once Stibbe has labelled his opponents as 'religious', he can play on this association in order to parallel them with Jesus' opponents and so charge them with blaspheming against the Holy Spirit.

The crucial thing to realise is that the teachers of the law and the Pharisees who opposed Jesus (and by no means all of them did) were opposing him *not* because they were 'religious' (whatever that means), but because Jesus was threatening their power-base. Jesus was raising up a movement of people who had previously been loyal to them. If the movement continued to grow the Roman authorities would begin to take notice and might then crack down on all Jews. Indeed they might conclude that the Pharisees were not worthy of their powerful position within Jewish society, since they were unable to control their followers.

Thus, Mt. 12.14 tells us that after Jesus had carried out the seemingly rebellious act of healing a man on the sabbath, 'the Pharisees went out and took counsel against him, how to destroy him'. The very next time the Pharisees are mentioned, ten verses later, they accuse Jesus of casting out demons by demonic power. It is clear this accusation came not out of 'religious' concern but out of a political desire for self-preservation. To be sure, their accusations against Jesus were religious in form, but they were made for non-religious reasons. These Pharisees were implacably opposed to Jesus. It seems to me they could hardly be more different from most of the critics of the 'Toronto Blessing', who are committed to serving their Lord Jesus Christ.

This brings us to the specific question of blasphemy. The Pharisees of Matthew 12 sought to destroy Jesus by whatever means could find. So when they saw Jesus heal a blind and dumb demoniac (v. 22) they brought their accusation. They knew the man had been healed. They knew Jesus had done a good thing. Yet they called it evil; they accused Jesus of satanic action. This was blasphemy, for it was God himself at work—not Satan. Blasphemy against the Holy Spirit should therefore be defined as 'calling works which are *known* to be of the Holy Spirit demonic'. This is the unforgivable sin. It is unforgivable because those who commit it are implacably opposed to Jesus' being Lord over them.

They wish, like some of those Pharisees, to maintain their own power-bases, and they are prepared even to call what they know to be good 'evil' for their own benefit. Such people have given themselves over to evil. So, immediately after his declaration about the unforgivable sin, Jesus speaks these words:

> *Either make the tree good, and its fruit good; or make the tree bad, and its fruit bad; for the tree is known by its fruit. You brood of vipers! How can you speak good, when you are evil? For out of the abundance of the heart the mouth speaks. The good man out of his good treasure brings forth good, and the evil man out of his evil treasure brings forth evil* (Mt. 12.33-35).

It is surely clear, therefore, that blasphemy against the Holy Spirit is the act of *knowingly* calling good bad or, more specifically, knowingly calling the works of the Holy Spirit demonic. It is equally clear to me that the majority of critics of the 'Blessing' do not do that. Rather, they genuinely believe (rightly or wrongly) that the phenomena of the 'Blessing' are not works of the Spirit. This is true even of those who call the 'Blessing' demonic. They call it demonic because they sincerely believe (in my view, wrongly) that it is so. Stibbe, therefore, should not hold the big stick of 'blasphemy' over his opponents. For what it is worth, I also believe, due to the seriousness of the accusation, he should publicly retract it.

The 'Gamaliel Principle'

But a Pharisee in the council named Gamaliel, a teacher of the law, held in honour by all the people, stood up and ordered the men to be put outside for a while. And he said to them, 'Men of Israel, take care what you do with these men...[K]eep away from these men and let them alone; for if this plan or this undertaking is of men, it will fail; but if it is of God, you will not be able to overthrow them. You might even be found opposing God!'   (Acts 5.34-35, 38-39)

I suspect that most critics of the 'Toronto Blessing' earnestly wish they could, in good conscience, follow the principle derived from these verses (that it is wisest not to criticise something if there is a chance it is 'of God'). They would prefer to keep quiet and carry on with their normal Christian lives. But the fact of the matter is that the 'Gamaliel Principle' does not apply.

The first point to make is that it is extremely unlikely that Luke (the writer of Acts) recorded Gamaliel's words in order for them to be adopted as a principle which Christians should follow. It is much more likely that Luke recorded them in support of one of the key themes of his book, that Christianity is the right and proper fulfilment of Jewish religion. An example of this theme is found in details Luke records about Paul. Howard Marshall notes that Paul, even after his conversion to Christianity,

> is presented as a law-abiding Jewish worshipper. ... [t]hat Paul was simply worshipping and serving God in the way that had been laid down in the Old Testament, and that he was and remained a Pharisee in his true convictions. In other words, *Christianity is true Judaism*.[7]

Luke recorded Gamaliel's reasoning in order to strengthen his point. In effect, Luke is saying, 'Look, even one of the most respected of the Jewish leaders believed that if Christianity succeeded it would be because the God of the Jews had caused it to succeed; and so it truly would be a religion supported by the Jewish God, it would be Jewish religion'. This is why Luke tells us about Gamaliel's reasoning.

Nevertheless, even if Luke did not intend Gamaliel's reasoning to become a general principle, is it a wise example for us to follow when considering the 'Toronto Blessing'? I believe it is not for two reasons.

First, the problem that Gamaliel faced was very different from ours. It was the problem of whether he and the other Jewish leaders should take advantage of the opportunity they appeared to have to put down an embryonic religious movement by force. They were deciding whether to put the leaders of this new movement to death. This is hardly the situation which critics of the 'Toronto Blessing' are in! Rather they are seeking to bring proper Christian criticism of some activities which other Christians are engaged in. I see no real parallel between this and Gamaliel's situation.

Second, while it is true that when God does something it cannot fail (though it may appear to do so for a time, as the cross bears witness), the opposite is not true. It is not true that when God is *not* behind something it inevitably fails. There have been countless religious movements which have sprung up throughout history. Indeed, the number of supposedly *Christian* movements that have appeared in the last two centuries alone is bewildering. Many of these movements draw Christians into heresy and damaging practices. Many of them succeed. It is my conviction that, if we allow such movements to go unchallenged, we fail in our duty to warn our fellow human beings against involvement with them.

By this I do not mean to imply, here and now, that the 'Blessing' is heretical or necessarily damaging. I am simply pointing out why the 'Gamaliel Principle' does not apply to this issue. It may be that there are occasions when members of governments would be wise to follow Gamaliel's reasoning, but Christians concerned with the state of the church cannot afford to do so. They must be wise according to 'Christian principles', not 'Gamaliel's Principle'.

Conclusion

In this chapter I have set out the reasons why I think there is room for proper Christian criticism of the 'Toronto Blessing'. I have described where I think there is room within the ongoing life of the 'priesthood of all believers' for criticism of beliefs adhered to and practices going on in the name of Christ. I have also described where I think there is room for the 'prophetic' type of criticism. Some critics of the 'Blessing' may see themselves more in that light. Finally, I have explained why I think it inappropriate to describe critics of the 'Blessing' as critics of God. As I have already said, none of us can be completely sure we are right. In the end, it may turn out we were wrong. At this stage we can do only what we believe to be right. We must do so before God, in the knowledge that he is our judge—but we must nonetheless do so.

NOTES
1. Mark Stibbe *Times of Refreshing* (London: Marshall Pickering, 1995), p. 173.
2. Ibid, p. 176.
3. Ibid, p. 177.
4. Ibid, p. 173.
5. Ibid, p. 176.
6. Idem.
7. I.H. Marshall, *Acts* (TNTC; IVP: Leicester, 1980), p. 28 (his italics).

CHAPTER 2

Is it Biblical?

Is it biblical? This is a question that will have crossed the mind of virtually every Christian who has come into contact with the 'Toronto Blessing'. It is certainly a question raised in almost every Christian article and book about the 'Blessing'. The leaders of the Toronto Vineyard church themselves asked (and answered) the question almost straight away, releasing a paper in May 1994 as 'a biblical apologetic for what we see happening among us'.[1]

Many of these articles and books conclude that the 'Blessing' is indeed biblical. And virtually all the church leaders involved in the 'Blessing' seem to agree. So, the average Christian might be forgiven for assuming that the question has been asked and answered satisfactorily. In my experience, however most of those involved have not checked for themselves that the 'Blessing' is biblical, but have merely assumed it on the say-so of others.

In September 1994 I refused to do that. As I have mentioned, at the time I was a member of a church which had thoroughly embraced the 'Blessing'. The church's main pastor repeatedly claimed that it was biblical. In 'Blessing' ministry times he read out lists of verses ostensibly demonstrated its biblical nature. I decided to check out those verses for myself. I concluded they could not be applied to the 'Blessing'. I have subsequently examined every text which—to my knowledge—has been raised in support of the

'Blessing'. The results of this are set out in Appendix 1, where each text is considered in detail. Here I will set out a representative sample of the type of Bible interpretation to be found in the various books and articles.

Strange Phenomena

The most obvious feature of the 'Toronto Blessing', and the one about which there has been the most controversy, is the occurrence of strange physical phenomena during and sometimes after meetings. Because it is the most obvious feature, a good deal of time has been spent in concordance and computer searches looking for similar phenomena in the Bible. The 'Blessing' phenomena have been put into the following categories: 1. falling down; 2. shaking/trembling; 3. 'drunkenness'; 4. involuntary weeping; 5. ecstatic laughter; 6. jumping up and down (pogo-ing); 7. jerking; 8. animal and other noises. This list is not exhaustive, but it includes those phenomena which have been most commonly seen up to this point.

Proponents tend to claim that categories 1 to 5 all occur in the Bible, while 6 and 7 do not. There is considerable controversy about category 8, with some saying it is biblical and others saying it is not. In fact, as Appendix 1 shows, the majority of verses that have been quoted in support of categories 1 to 5 simply cannot be applied to the 'Toronto Blessing'. This is usually because, although the verse might speak, for example, of someone falling down or trembling, a look at the context shows that what is meant is nothing like the current 'Blessing' phenomena.

Trembling and Shaking

One example will suffice to explain what I mean. A text commonly cited in support of Toronto-type shaking is Jer. 5.22a: "'Do you not fear me? says the LORD; Do you not tremble before me?'" At first sight, this verse may seem quite plausible. After all, in 'Blessing' meetings the Holy Spirit is usually invited to come, and people do often start to tremble. Is this not the trembling before the Lord of Jer. 5.22a? The answer has to be, No. The context of the verse is a command from the Lord to Jeremiah to say to his fellow Jews,

> *'Hear this, O foolish and senseless people, who have eyes, but see not, who have ears, but hear not. Do you not fear me?' says the LORD; 'Do you not tremble before me? I placed the sand as the bound for the sea, a perpetual barrier which it cannot pass; though the waves toss, they cannot prevail, though they roar, they cannot pass over it. But this people has a stubborn and rebellious heart; they have turned aside and gone away. They do not say in their hearts, 'Let us fear the LORD our God, who gives the rain in its season, the autumn rain and the spring rain, and keeps for us the weeks appointed for the harvest.' Your iniquities have turned these away, and your sins have kept good from you.'*

Here we find God calling his people to repent of the terrible sins they have been committing and to return to a proper fear of their Lord and Creator. The question, 'Do you not tremble before me?' is a rhetorical one. In effect, it is saying, 'You are at this moment sinning against me and I have it in my power to do away with you. If you realised the precarious nature of your situation you would be trembling in fear.'

Now it seems to me that if Jer. 5.22a were to be applied today, it would be in the following sort of situation: A modern-day Jeremiah would declare to people in the church who are sinning, perhaps by exploiting poor and needy people in order to become rich (see Jer. 5.26-28), that they are doing wrong and that they should stand in fear of God punishing them (see Jer. 5.29). Jer. 5.22a in other words, is a verse which can be applied to a situation in which there is a call for repentance of serious wrong-doing and for a return to the fear of the Lord.

This is most emphatically not what is going on in the 'Toronto Blessing'. In his book *Catch the Fire*[2], Guy Chevreau supplies fifteen representative testimonies of people who have experienced the 'Blessing'. In four of them, the person testifying experienced trembling/shaking. None of the four mentions feeling fear that God will punish them, or a need to repent of wrong-doing. In fact, what they tend to describe are positive feelings accompanying the shaking. One felt an 'incredible peace'[3], another was laughing and shaking[4], another believed she was being healed.[5]

The paper 'What in the World is Happening to us?', supplied by the Toronto Vineyard church, backs up this evidence that Toronto-type trembling/shaking appears to involve something other than the fear of God recorded in Jer. 5.22. The writer says,

> There is a biblical precedent for shaking in God's presence. In the verses where the cause of shaking is mentioned, it has to do with holy fear. The shaking we are experiencing seems to be related more to prophetic ministry and impartation of spiritual gifts.[6]

Unfortunately, the author of the paper fails to follow the logic of his own argument, and so he does not admit that, while there is indeed 'a biblical precedent for shaking in God's presence' there is *not* a biblical precedent for Toronto-type shaking. Indeed, this is representative of the failure of all the attempts I have seen to demonstrate the presence of 'Toronto Blessing' phenomena in the Bible.

Before we move on from this section, it is worth considering the fourth of the testimonies about shaking which I mentioned above. I believe it is typical of a great deal that has been experienced in the 'Blessing'. It is the testimony of a man who is musical director for two Baptist churches and one Presbyterian church in Canada. Here is an extract of what he says:

> When I was prayed for at the Vineyard, the work of God in my life speeded up at an incredible rate. I had been growing in the gift of prophecy before I went, but afterwards the gift has become much more powerful. There are now physical manifestations that accompany the original gifting, *stirred up to such an extent that the power is so strong, my limbs shake with it!* I am thankful not so much for the new manifestations, as for the new power.
>
> For some people the manifestations might be something highly desirable. This has not been the case for me. The manifestations have been very awkward and humbling. In the conservative circles in which I move, it is very troublesome to have dramatic manifestations accompanying your ministry! For example, shortly after I was prayed for, I sat at my computer typing the church bulletin, and in the course of copying the order of service, I typed the words, 'Come, Holy Spirit'. *I was immediately thrown into a fit of shaking, and bounced around on my wheeled office chair!* These sorts of manifestations are often intrusive! I have had to learn to laugh and thank God for them.[7]

I have highlighted in italics what this man specifically says about his experience of shaking. This is not to ignore the rest of what he says. It should be taken very seriously, as should the fact that for him the experience has been a positive Christian one. I will return to this in a while, but for the moment I want to focus on what he specifically says about his shaking.

Notice, the shaking is a result of a sensation of power flooding his body and, as far as he can tell, this comes to him rather than being something he has caused himself. One point arising from this is that, without saying just what this *is*, we can say it is definitely *not* trembling as a result of fear of God's judgement, such as we read of in Jer. 5.22a. The trembling is simply something 'happening to' the man. According to his testimony, he does not feel any fear at all. The second point is a very interesting one. From the many testimonies I have read and heard, it seems that, in general, the 'strange phenomena' are caused by sensations within, which people are not aware of causing themselves. The sensations are quite varied and result in varied physical effects. So, for example, a sensation of power leads to shaking/trembling, a sensation of loss of strength leads to falling down. Other sensations lead to ecstatic laughter, uncontrollable weeping and so on. These sensations are what we might call 'non-cognitive'. That is, they do not involve conscious thought. The person is almost always able to think, but their thoughts may be entirely unrelated to the sensation, or else they will be thoughts *about* the sensation.

Non-cognitive Experience

Put another way, the majority of the phenomena are not caused by such things as visions or 'messages in the head'. This is not to deny that there have been such visions and messages. But, according to the reports, they usually come separately from the physical phenomena and in any case are in the minority. Much more common is the following sort of non-cognitive experience:

> ...we were about to go home when one of them asked if he could pray for me. I said, "Sure, but I must tell you I've been prayed for many times." I didn't want him to get his hopes up.
>
> Within a minute or so, suddenly my mind became so relaxed. The nearest I can think of to describe it was when I had sodium pentathol years ago when I had major surgery.
>
> Yet I wasn't unconscious. I felt myself falling forward.
>
> [The interviewer asked,] Did he have a great sense of God? 'No more than I had all day; it had been a great day for me.'
>
> What, then, was the meaning of this experience? 'For me it was so humbling. I think God was wanting to teach me to be humbled, to look stupid and be a fool. There I was on the floor in front of all my deacons and their wives.'[8]

Notice how the experience itself does not involve the mind, it is non-cognitive. It was only afterwards, when he thought about the experience, that this man came to think of it as having meaning, specifically of being humbling.

For the moment I want to leave open the question of what causes these sensations—perhaps the Holy Spirit, perhaps something else. What I want to do here is establish two rather more mundane points. First, it is fair to describe the 'Toronto Blessing' as a movement in which people experience inward, non-cognitive sensations which they do not believe to be self-induced. Second, when we describe the 'Blessing' in this way, we can see there is no real biblical precedent for it. To be sure, there are (fairly rare) occasions when people fall down in the Bible. But on those occasions there are significant differences from what seems to be typical falling down in the 'Toronto Blessing'. I deal with the detail of these occasions in Appendix 1. We can say here, though, that the majority of falling cases in the 'Toronto Blessing' seem to lack the key feature of the biblical cases—namely, some sort of vision of God. Instead, the falling seems to be in some kind of 'switched off' state in which people 'feel good', 'happy' and so on.

It is not my purpose to deny such experiences, only to point out that they are not the same as those found in the Bible. It is also significant that the majority of the cases of falling down in the Bible are occasions where a person or persons are confronted by one greater than themselves (often God or an angel of God) and in response cast themselves down in fear and worship. There is no indication in these cases that God's Spirit directly causes the falling down by doing something strange to their bodies.

To take another phenomenon, there are plenty of occasions where people laugh in the Bible. But again, they laugh for a reason—the experience has cognitive content. There is no sense in the Bible of people being made to laugh ecstatically for no outward reason.

With the vast majority of 'strange phenomena' in the Bible there is no evidence of God giving people inward, non-cognitive sensations. Perhaps someone might point to the occasion when God caused Adam to fall into a deep sleep so he could form Eve out of Adam's side. This, however, seems to be an exception which proves the rule. The general rule is that when, in the Bible, God does something with his people, it is first and foremost cognitive or physical. God speaks, or shows somebody something, or does something physical such as a nature miracle or a healing. All of these ways of God acting are what we might call 'biblical'. But the strange phenomena of the 'Toronto Blessing' do not appear to fit into any of these categories. Of course, none of this proves that the 'Blessing' phenomena are wrong or not 'of God'. But it does lead to the conclusion that the attempt to show they are biblical in the sense of being found in the Bible has failed.

The 'Blessing' Itself

A second strand of the attempt to show that the 'Toronto Blessing' is truly Christian is the argument that the movement as a whole is biblical. This is different from the argument that the assorted phenomena can be found in various Bible texts. Rather it is a claim that the Bible *predicts* movements such as the 'Blessing'.

Acts 3.19

For many Christians, no matter which physical phenomena they have experienced, their involvement in the 'Blessing' has provided a time of fresh enjoyment and excitement about being a Christian. Many previously had felt 'spiritually fatigued', even depressed about their faith, and the 'Blessing' turned this situation around. The word which seems to encapsulate all this for them is 'refreshing'. And so Acts 3.19, which contains the phrase 'times of refreshing', is cited. The claim is that, through the 'Toronto Blessing', God is 'refreshing' Christians (it is often added that he is doing this in preparation for a time of revival) and that the refreshing is predicted in Acts 3.19.

There is no need to dispute that this feeling of refreshment is very real for many. Later, I will offer my own evaluation of it. At this point, however, what we need to ask is whether Acts 3.19 can justifiably be applied to it. The best way to answer the question is to forget for a moment the kind of 'refreshing' people get from the 'Blessing' and consider what the passage in which the verse is contained tells us about 'times of refreshing'. Once we know that, we can consider whether it is the same sort of thing as is being experienced now. The verse is part of a speech given by Peter to non-Christian Jews. He says,

> *'Repent therefore, and turn again, that your sins may be blotted out, that times of refreshing may come from the presence of the Lord'.*

Peter is speaking about something which the Lord will do once the Jews he is addressing turn to God in repentance. It is something which will come, in other words, when they convert; when they become Christians. What is it the Lord will do? Two things are closely related in verse 19. The Lord will blot out the sins of those who convert and he will give 'times of refreshing'.

The phrase 'times of refreshing' is best understood against the background of the experience of the Jewish people just prior to and during the life of Jesus. This historical background helps us appreciate what the people listening to Peter's speech understood him to mean. Briefly, Jews had been living the hard life of an oppressed people: their land was occupied by Roman forces, they paid taxes to Caesar and their religious and legal freedom was considerably curtailed. Their hope was that God would send a messiah to lead them in a victorious war, freeing them from the Romans. Such a war would be followed by respite from the hardships they had suffered.

In the Greek translation of the Hebrew Scriptures, known as the Septuagint, which was the most popular version of their Scriptures for many of the Jews of the time, the only occurrence of the word *anapsucheos* (translated 'refreshing' in Acts 3.19) is Exod. 8.15, where 'Pharaoh saw that there was a respite' (Greek: *anapsuchis*) from the plague of frogs. It is possible therefore that by 'times of refreshing' Peter was referring to respite from God's judgement on unrepentant Israel.

Whether Peter was specifically thinking of the Septuagint translation of Exod. 8.15 or not, it seems sure that he was referring to the Jewish hope for freedom from the Romans. However, with the coming of Jesus—God's true messiah—Peter and the other disciples had been brought to understand that God was giving them a spiritual freedom, not a nationalistic, military one. This is true of Jesus' preaching of the kingdom, which would at first have been understood in a military sense by his hearers, but which Jesus intended in a spiritual sense. The disciples had to come to understand that Jesus was offering a different definition of the concept of 'kingdom' to the one they had held. In my view, Peter is doing the same with the concept of 'times of refreshing': the refreshing was to be spiritual, not material. Peter promises his hearers that, when they convert, God will give them spiritual freedom, freedom from the oppression of sin and demonic forces. He may well also be thinking of physical healing, since his speech is given on the occasion of the healing of a man lame from birth.

Therefore, the best way of applying Acts 3.19 to today is to say that by 'times of refreshing' it promises all the spiritual benefits which result from life in Christ; these 'refresh' us after the hardness of our previous life in which we were 'dead in our sins'. It is speaking of something which has been happening throughout all of the two thousand years since Christ died for our sins. It is speaking of the glorious new life of freedom which comes to each of us as we turn to Jesus Christ.

For the sake of completeness, it is worth noting that there is an alternative, perhaps complementary, possible interpretation of 'times of refreshing'. This interpretation focuses more strongly on the note of impending judgement in Peter's speech. Peter declares that God had sent Jesus as a saviour, but, 'you denied the Holy and Righteous One, and asked for a murderer to be granted to you, and killed the Author of life, whom God raised from the dead' (vv. 14-15). As a result, his hearers deserve only punishment (see v. 23). However, if they will repent, 'respite' (*anapsucheos*) from the coming punishment is possible (vv. 19-20). According to this interpretation, therefore, 'times of refreshing' has more to do with relief from deserved punishment than with receiving spiritual benefits. Historically speaking, the Jewish nation as a whole did not repent and turn to Jesus as their saviour. Many people see the fall of Jerusalem just a few years later in AD 70 as the resultant judgement and punishment.

We are in a good position now to consider how Acts 3.19 relates to the 'Toronto Blessing'. If my interpretation is correct, then it cannot be maintained that the verse predicts special moves of God, such as the 'Blessing' is taken to be. Instead it predicts what happens each time a person becomes a Christian. (Even if my interpretation is rejected in favour of the alternative I have outlined, it remains fallacious to apply the verse to the 'Blessing', since *respite from punishment* is not the same thing as *blessing*.)

An appeal to the Greek text, such as Mark Stibbe makes in his book *Times of Refreshing* does not overturn this. Stibbe is wrong to claim that what 'is occurring in Toronto and throughout the world is THAT articulated by Peter in Acts 3'. The Greek words in question are *kairoi anapsucheos*, about which he says,

> The word *kairos* denotes a sovereignly ordained season, a unique period of time which is planned by God. We should note that the word is in the plural, *kairoi*, and that Peter is therefore speaking of more than one such season. *Anapsucheos* is the genitive singular of *anapsuchis*, a noun rarely used in the New Testament but which literally means 'a breathing space', 'a short time of relief and relaxation'. In a figurative sense this word is used by Peter in Acts 3:19 to refer to seasons of rest and renewal during the Messianic Age.[11]

Here is an example of somebody mistakenly making too much from definitions of words and paying too little attention to their context. It is important that we do not make too much of simple definitions of words, because it is possible for a writer to mean something other than the 'dictionary definition'. This is particularly the case when we study ancient documents—such as Acts—when dictionaries did not exist. Of course, lexicographical definitions are helpful, but the immediate context must always have the final say in determining what a word means. This is especially so with a rare word such as *anapsuchis*.

It seems most likely that Peter uses the phrase *kairoi anapsucheos* because it was already used by Jews to describe their hoped-for freedom from foreign oppression. He in turn re-defines it as freedom from spiritual oppression. Consequently, it is wrong to lend the literal meaning so much weight. With regard to *kairos*, it is true that it usually means 'a unique period of time which is planned by God' and that it is plural in Acts 3.19b, but this fits perfectly well with the interpretation I have offered. When a person becomes a Christian they do so in 'a unique period of time which is planned by God', and, because many have become Christians, there have been many such times.

It is my contention, therefore, that Acts 3.19 cannot be applied to the 'Toronto Blessing' in the way Stibbe and others suggest. It does not predict specific periods in history when God will give great numbers of Christians feelings of refreshment. Rather, it speaks of God's action throughout the whole of history as he gives spiritual blessings to every person who becomes a Christian. In this very much weaker sense it may be possible to say that Acts 3.19 does apply to what is happening in some people's lives. If they truly have received blessings from God (and this is a question I have yet to address), then they have received part of their 'time of refreshing'. However, this weaker sense is not what the 'Blessing's' supporters are arguing for, since it would not enable them to say the movement itself is biblical.

Ezekiel 47

Consequently, some people add another strand to the argument. They claim Ezekiel 47, read in a particular way, also predicts the 'Toronto Blessing'. Again Mark Stibbe is representative of this view. It is what he calls 'the THIS is THAT' view. 'This', which we are seeing now in the 'Toronto Blessing', is 'that' which is promised in Ezekiel 47.

Ezekiel 47 contains a vision of a river flowing out from Israel's temple. As the river leaves the temple, it is described in four stages. In the first stage, nearest to the temple, the water is ankle-deep. As it flows further it becomes knee-deep, then waist deep, before finally becoming too deep to touch the bottom. Stibbe says,

> I would like to propose ... the following thesis: that in the twentieth century, we can speak of four main movements of God's Holy Spirit, and that these four 'waves' represent a THIS which corresponds to the THAT which we find in Ezekiel 47:1-12.[12]

The first wave in the twentieth century, he says, was the emergence of Pentecostalism in 1906. Then came the Charismatic Renewal in the 1960s, followed by what he calls the 'Protestant Evangelical Renewal' in the 1980s sparked by John Wimber. Soon a fourth wave will emerge of which 'the Toronto phenomenon is the first sign'.[13] These four waves, in Stibbe's view, correspond to the four stages of the river in Ezekiel 47.

Many Christians will find this an extraordinary and unacceptable way of treating the Bible. I agree with them. There are enormous *hermeneutical* difficulties with Stibbe's position which space does not permit us to deal with here. Instead, we will consider only the specific details of his interpretation of Ezekiel's vision.

Stibbe does admit 'there are obviously a couple of large claims within this thesis'.[14] The first is that there have indeed been three waves of the Spirit this century and that there is a fourth one coming. He considers this claim 'to be historically sound'.[15] I am not a church historian, so I will not debate that assertion here. It is the second 'large claim' which I want to concentrate on: the claim that what we have seen in the twentieth century is the 'That' of Ezekiel 47. Stibbe admits that this is 'a claim which is much harder to sustain on academic and intellectual grounds.' However, he does not think that this is too important because, '[i]n matters such as these we enter the realm of the prophetic, and academic scholarship has a poor track record when it comes to understanding and uttering prophecy.'[16]

At this stage we need to ask two important questions. What is meant by 'the realm of the prophetic'? And, on what grounds does Stibbe think his claim can be sustained?

First then, does Stibbe mean that when we try to interpret Ezekiel 47 we are interpreting a prophetic book, and academic scholarship has usually offered rather poor treatments of such books? Or, alternatively, does he mean that the particular interpretation he is offering is prophetic, and academic scholarship is bad at dealing with such interpretations? There may be an element of the former in what he says (though he does not make it very clear), but it seems the latter predominates in his thinking. Stibbe considers himself as being prophetic in his interpretation of Ezekiel 47. Thus he speaks of the 'THIS-IS-THAT' approach to the Bible as coming out of 'a prophetic sense' which comes to the 'Spirit-filled interpreter'.[17] In support of his interpretation he notes the remarkable 'coincidence' that, a few weeks before he preached a sermon based on his interpretation, somebody else had preached at the same church a very similar sermon based on Ezekiel 47. A number of people had come up to him after the sermon and told him this, and then asked,

> 'What's going on?!' To which I replied, 'What's going on is that two people may be hearing similar things from the Lord.'[18]

We have, then, the answer to our first question, What is meant by 'the realm of the prophetic'? Stibbe means he is offering a prophetic interpretation which was given to him by the Holy Spirit. This in turn offers us a provisional answer to our second question, On what grounds does Stibbe think his claim can be sustained? He believes the claim that the 'this' going on now is the 'that' of Ezekiel 47 can be sustained on the grounds that God gave him the interpretation. This leads to the conclusion that its status is the same as that given to prophecies offered by charismatic and pentecostal Christians all over the world regularly. So Stibbe advises his post-sermon questioners,

What you need to do is to test and see.[19]

We should be absolutely clear that this 'prophetic interpretation' of Ezekiel 47 cannot be offered by proponents of the 'Toronto Blessing' as proof that the *Bible* prophesies the 'Blessing' or teaches that it is of God. It is the people who offer the interpretation—such as Stibbe—who are speaking, they think, prophetically. They are making use of words and pictures taken from the Bible as a part of their own prophecies, but it is not the Bible that is speaking. This, of course, goes on in countless churches all over the world. There is nothing wrong with such symbolism in and of itself. Many excellent, truly edifying prophecies have been given which use biblical language and imagery. (This does not alter the fact that it is wrong for somebody to claim that the use of such language proves the content of the prophecy to be biblical and of God—many prophecies have been given which are expressed in biblical language but which are not inspired by the Holy Spirit.) Yet such prophecies must be tested. Traditionally, pentecostals and charismatics have argued that we must consider whether prophecies are 'biblical'. That is, their content must be in accord with biblical principles.

To return to the detail of the Ezekiel 47 interpretation, somebody might say that, although the interpretation originally came prophetically, now that it has been offered, what is going on in the 'Blessing' does seem just like what is spoken of in the text. Stibbe, for example, says something like this. There is a pattern, he thinks, set out in Ezekiel 47, which is being repeated in this century. It is a pattern of the way the Holy Spirit works in renewal. He admits that the Spirit does not have to stick to this pattern, for 'the ways of the Spirit are mysterious; they are like the desert wind in ancient Palestine (John 3:8).' But then he says,

> At the very least, we can speak of a pattern of renewal portrayed in the Ezekiel text, a pattern involving four mighty and miraculous effusions of the Spirit from the heart of the Divine Presence. That ... is a symbolic picture of what I believe has been happening (and indeed *is* happening) in the twentieth century.[20]

At this point Stibbe is not simply offering his own prophecy in which he merely makes use of the text. He is asserting that the text itself teaches something, namely a pattern for renewal. He is also asserting that the 'Toronto Blessing' fits into this pattern.

Therefore we need to ask, does Ezekiel 47 actually offer a fourfold pattern for renewal? Ironically enough, although he fails to realise it, Stibbe's own exegesis of the chapter shows it does not. He tells us that when he first studied this passage three years ago and was struck by his sense of 'this' is 'that',

> it was the number four which attracted my attention. Ezekiel has a fondness for that particular number: it occurs 40 times in the book. As early as Ezekiel 1:5 we are introduced to four living creatures.

There are four main visions of Ezekiel as a whole. Four seems to be a key number. Why?

His answer is significant.

Because in Ezekiel's time it was a number *which symbolized totality or completeness.* Hence Ezekiel 37:9: 'Come from the four winds, O breath!' i.e. come from every corner of the earth. [21]

This is absolutely correct. The number four does symbolise totality or completeness. But that ruins Stibbe's argument. The vision of the river in Ezekiel 47 is not intended to symbolise four literal stages of renewal. Stibbe pushes the details of the vision too far. Just as the four winds of Ezek. 37.9 do not symbolise the breath of God coming in four stages, but rather coming *from everywhere*, so the four depths (not waves, by the way!) of the river symbolise that *complete* renewal will come. It is 'over-interpretation' (reading too much out of the text) to claim anything more. The completeness is emphasised by the fact that when the river of Ezekiel 47 reaches its fourth stage, it is a river through which Ezekiel cannot pass (v. 5) and everywhere it goes it brings life.

It too much to claim that the text sets out a pattern for the way things will actually happen. The text promises complete renewal, and symbolises this by the number four. It does not promise four actual stages to renewal. Claiming that is like claiming there really are four winds or four corners of the earth. In fact, it is the same kind of mistake made by Jehovah's Witnesses regarding the 144,000 in Rev. 7.4. This number is symbolic of the enormous number of people saved by God and sealed safe from his wrath. But Jehovah's Witnesses have taken the number literally, thinking that only 144,000 people will finally attain everlasting life (the fact that there are now more than 144,000 Jehovah's Witnesses has caused them to begin modifying this claim).

These considerations are enough to show that Ezekiel 47 has been misinterpreted, and consequently that it is wrong to claim the 'Toronto Blessing' is biblical in this sense.

Conclusion

All sides in the debate must agree, I think, that the most distinctive feature of the 'Toronto Blessing' is the enormous number of strange physical phenomena occurring with it. It is this which makes it different. It is this which has aroused the curiosity of the world's media, and has made it a distinctive movement in today's church.

It is certainly true that the Bible contains a number of instances of strange physical phenomena. But, as we have seen, there are significant differences between the biblical phenomena and the 'Blessing' phenomena. These differences make it impossible to substantiate the claim that what is happening now is the same as what happened in the Bible. In that sense, therefore, it is wrong to claim the 'Toronto Blessing' is biblical. We have also seen that it is wrong to claim it is biblical in the second sense of being a move of God predicted in the Bible, either on the basis of Ezekiel 47 or of Acts 3. The Bible contains the phrase 'times of refreshing' in Acts 3, but this does not justify the claim that this particular text is a prediction of the current movement simply because people are experiencing 'refreshing'.

So, the answer to the question in this Chapter's title is, No, the 'Toronto Blessing' is not biblical in the sense of being 'found in the Bible' or 'predicted by the Bible'.

NOTES
1. B. Jackson, 'What in the World is Happening to Us? A Biblical Perspective on Renewal', (May, 1994). The paper has been reprinted at the end of Patrick Dixon's book, *Signs of Revival* (Kingsway, Eastbourne 1995). Presumably, Dixon considers it to provide biblical grounding for the phenomena.
2. Guy Chevreau, *Catch the Fire* (London: Marshall Pickering, 1994).
3. Ibid, p. 156.
4. Ibid, p. 167.
5. Ibid, p. 171.
6. 'What in World is happening to us?', p. 6.
7. *Catch the Fire*, p. 192.
8. From Renewal magazine, October 1994 issue, p. 13.
9. Idem
10. London: Marshall Pickering, 1995.
11. *Times of Refreshing*, p. 171.
12. Ibid, p. 10.
13. Idem.
14. Idem.
15. Idem.
16. Idem.
17. Ibid, p. 7.
18. Ibid, pp. 6-7.
19. Ibid, p. 7.
20. Ibid, pp. 10-11.
21. Ibid, p. 9.

CHAPTER 3

Is it 'Non-Biblical'?

The simple fact that something is neither found in, nor predicted by, the Bible, does not necessarily make it wrong. Supporters of the 'Toronto Blessing' rightly point out there are all kinds of activities Christians engage in that are not strictly biblical. We build church buildings, have hymn books and overhead projectors, run youth clubs, and so on. Obviously it is narrow and legalistic to disallow something purely on the basis that it is not in the Bible. If we did, we would have to disallow a whole range of things, from medicine to worship bands.

The well-known house church leader Gerald Coates has used this argument in support of the 'Blessing'. He points out that,

> the Bible is not given so that we can provide a proof text for everything. Most Christians are currently engaged in a wide range of church activities for which there are no proof texts ... God wants us to grow up. Between those things he specifically approves of, and others he specifically disapproves of, we are given liberty to develop a wide range of activities broadly to reflect things he approves of.[1]

He calls these activities which reflect things God approves of, 'non-biblical'.

Coates' point is valid. The Bible should not be used simply as a proof-text, and there are many things we rightly do which are not found in the Bible. But does that help? It does, but only if we are able to go on and judge whether those activities are good, bad or indifferent. We do indeed need to 'grow up', as Coates puts it. Yet he does not seem to see the force of his own argument! It is as though, for him, the image of growing up means only liberty. But growing up, as well as liberating us to do things without our parents' specific permission, involves us not doing things which our parents can no longer stop us from doing: for example, when we grow up we should choose not to lie and cheat, though we have no-one to tell us not to.

Responsible Interpretation

This is a crucial matter. If we accept that some things are 'non-biblical', then we must be prepared to wrestle with whether they are good, bad or indifferent; whether they are 'biblical' in the wider sense; whether as Christians we should be involved in them or not. If something really is 'non-biblical', then the need for responsible Bible interpretation is all the greater. This is particularly so in the case of something having such enormous effects and making such enormous claims for itself as the 'Toronto Blessing'. Unfortunately, wrestling with these matters is rare, and instead the category of 'non-biblical' tends to be used as a 'get-out'. It is not enough to say that because the 'Blessing' is 'non-biblical' we have liberty to take it on board. *We have the responsibility to judge whether it accords with biblical principles.* To take Coates' analogy in the direction I believe it should properly go, we need to grow up and make responsible decisions.

It appears that at least some proponents of the 'Blessing' have made a dangerous move. They initially claimed that the 'Blessing' is in the Bible, and then, when challenged, they said that it does not matter if it is not there because there is a second category of 'non-biblical' that can be applied. This will not do. A person who seriously accepts that the 'Blessing' cannot be directly justified from the Bible should be prepared to get down to the hard work of judging it according to biblical principles.

Can God do anything?

There is a particular argument that often runs parallel with the 'non-biblical argument'. It goes along the lines of: 'You who are criticising are being narrow and legalistic and are trying to put God in a box; don't you know God can do anything, even things not in the Bible'. This sounds very convincing. But it is an argument which Christians should not use. Any argument which relies on the claim 'God can do anything' is relying on what used to be called 'pagan philosophy', not on biblical principles. A god who can 'do anything' is a god invented by philosophers—not the God of the Bible. The god of the philosophers, for example, could at any moment consign every human being who has ever existed to oblivion.

We know that the God of the Bible, on the other hand, will not do that. He has shown himself to be the God who will raise his children to eternal life. The God of the Bible has shown himself to be a God who acts in certain ways and not in others. The God of the Bible is a loving, faithful and consistent God; slow to anger and quick to mercy; a God who never acts capriciously or spitefully. The God of the Bible is the Almighty, Sovereign God; but he is not a god who will 'do anything'.

If, as Christians, we allow the argument 'God can do anything', we open ourselves up to all kinds of problems. For example, what if we were faced with a sect which believed it right to sacrifice babies? They might well justify their position by saying, 'God can do anything, including demanding the lives of new-born babies.' Or what if a sect claimed that God enables its members to levitate and go on 'astral trips' around the universe? Surely our proper response is to say that the God who has revealed himself in the Bible does not do these things.

It may be that the theoretical god of the philosophers, the god who can 'do anything', might well make a person jerk or shake or 'pogo-jump'; the question is whether the God of the Bible, the one true God, would do these things. It is a question that can only be answered by responsible Bible interpretation, and not by the rather dangerous claim, 'God can do anything'.

A Historical Comparison

To claim that the 'Toronto Blessing' is 'non-biblical' and leave it at that, is insufficient. Having said it is 'non-biblical', responsible Bible interpretation must be supplied to show why it is nonetheless right—or 'biblical'—in some broader sense. Until such an interpretation is supplied, those involved in the 'Blessing' do not have the right to claim that what they are doing is biblical.

It is instructive to compare the current state of affairs with what happened during the rise of Pentecostalism at the beginning of this century and the rise of the charismatic movement in the 1960s. There is an interesting comparison, in terms of Bible interpretation, between the beginnings of both Pentecostalism and of Charismatic Renewal and the beginnings of the 'Toronto Blessing'. It may be simplifying matters somewhat, but I think it is fair to say that both Pentecostalism and Charismatic Renewal began with people who read of spiritual gifts in the Bible, recognised that these were not a part of contemporary church life, and began praying that they would become so. These movements both arose therefore—at least in part—out of a realisation that something which was in the Bible, i.e. 'biblical', ought to become an active part of current Christian life. Indeed the same thing can be said about many important movements in church history: think of the Reformation, and Luther reading Paul's letter to the Romans; or think of Augustine and, later, Wesley, both of whom re-discovered the truths contained in the letter to the Romans.

Contrast that with the descriptions of how things happened in Toronto: the kinds of phenomena which began to break out were almost entirely unexpected. The leaders had been looking for something to begin happening, but it was not 'strange physical phenomena' that they were looking for and that they had somehow come to perceive in the Bible. In fact, recurring through the accounts of how the 'Blessing' got started are reports of how the leaders were looking for such things as 'spiritual boosts',[2] 'empowerment'[3] and 'power in ministry'.[4]

There is no reason to doubt that they sought these things out of good motives. Presumably they did not want power for its own sake, but because they thought it would promote God's kingdom. Nevertheless, there is a considerable difference between the way the 'Toronto Blessing' began and the way Pentecostalism and Charismatic Renewal began. That is, it can be said of Pentecostalism and

Charismatic Renewal that they were to some extent brought about by the Bible causing people to look for some sort of reform in church life. With the 'Toronto Blessing', however, its leaders looked for a manifestation of power; and they got it. Only later on did they go back to their Bibles and make efforts to justify it as 'biblical'.

It seems likely to me that sooner or later many ordinary Christians will come to realise, despite what their leaders have said, that the 'Toronto Blessing' is not present in the Bible, and that their leaders have failed to show that it is in line with biblical principles. Such Christians will then have to face the contradiction between this situation and their deeply held commitment to being 'biblical'. My fear is that many of them will be able to cope with such a contradiction only by giving up in disillusionment and disappointment—abandoning their churches and perhaps even Christianity as a whole. I pray this will not happen, but I fear it will.

In the meantime, it is important that those involved in the 'Blessing' (if they still believe Christianity should be 'biblical') stop and think about what they are doing. They should not be asking, 'Is what we are doing powerful?' Nor, 'Does what we are doing make people feel good or excited?' Nor even, 'Does it get them coming to more meetings?' There are plenty of experiences in this world which are powerful, and which make people feel good and excited and go to more meetings, and even want to tell their friends and neighbours about this 'powerful thing'. But these things are not necessarily Christian. There are mystics and gurus all around the world who do powerful deeds and get many excited, happy converts. People involved in the 'Toronto Blessing' must not ask, 'Is it powerful?' but, 'Is it biblical?' This chapter shows that the category of 'non-biblical' is not sufficient to enable them to answer 'Yes'.

Many supporters of the 'Blessing' realise that. There is another argument which they find much more convincing, indeed it sounds convincing to most people. It runs like this: though many of the strange physical phenomena are not in themselves biblical, the 'fruit' which is being produced *is* biblical. In this argument, the category of 'non-biblical' becomes useful again: jumping vigorously up and down on one spot for an extended period of time may indeed be 'non-biblical', but it produces wonderful fruit, and therefore it is to be welcomed. As Guy Chevreau puts it, 'having bounced, or better, been bounced, does the person love Jesus more?'[5] Look at the fruit, says Chevreau. If the fruit is good, then the 'non-biblical' things should be encouraged.

This clearly is a powerful argument, and we will consider it in detail in the next Chapter. To end this Chapter I want to look at something which is brought to light by my analysis of the concept of 'non-biblical' and which is found in much of the use of the Bible in today's churches. This is the tendency among many churches to use the Bible most of the time only as a kind of warning indicator. At the time of writing it is just a tendency, and few churches have taken it to its extreme, but it is worth taking note of.

Is the Bible just a Test Book?

Gerald Coates uses the catch-phrase, 'The Bible is not a text book, it is a test book.' He explains this statement by saying, 'We draw our experiences alongside Scripture to test them to see whether they are of God or not.'[6] What he means by saying 'The Bible is not a text book' is that we should not use it for proof-texting. I agree. But is it sufficient to say the Bible is a 'test book'? Certainly one way we should use the Bible is to test our experiences, but there is far more to it than that.

The logical implication of Coates' position is that our experiences do not need to have their source in the Bible so long as they do not actually contradict its principles. This reduces the function of the Bible to a rather limited one. It is like the rule book for a game in which the players are allowed to do anything they want except what is explicitly outlawed by the rules. Such a rule book does not tell the players how to play the game well, only what they are not allowed to do. Or it is like the smoke alarms many of us have in our houses. For the great majority of the time, smoke alarms have no influence at all over what goes on in our houses. Only when something goes wrong, when there is a fire, do they make any difference.

The Bible is far more than a rule book or a smoke alarm. It is more than a 'test book'. It is God's Word to us. It tells us about Jesus Christ, the one human being who lived as humans are supposed to live. And it tells us what God has done for us in and through Jesus Christ. Through it we can come to know how we should live and how we should behave in the enormously varied circumstances we each face. In this sense, 'our experiences' should have their source in the Bible.

I do not mean that we should shut ourselves away from modern life, with all its differences from life in Bible times. Far from it. What is wanted is Christians who feel able to throw themselves, with gusto, into modern life, because they are people who already know how to live; people who have heard God's Word, and so are able to be in the world but not of it. We should be people who find the source of our life in God's Word and so are not left floundering in a difficult, sometimes evil world. The Bible should not be merely a 'test book'. Instead it is the source, guide and control of both our individual and corporate life. If it is this then we will be able to be 'salt and light to the world', for we will be like Jesus.

If, on the other hand, the Bible remains merely a 'test book', we will be people whose lives seem to be little different from others' lives. Perhaps we will be a little more moral, for the Bible tells us not to be adulterers and thieves—though there are many people in the world who are just as moral as Christians. Perhaps we will be a little more giving, for the Bible tells us not to love material things— though, again, there are many charitable people in the world. But in essence we will seem pretty much the same as others, because the source for the way we live will be the same as it is for everybody else.

What / Who is the Holy Spirit?

Of course, some might object that the source of Christian life is the Holy Spirit, not a book. This is perfectly true: we are born anew by the Spirit of God and it is the Spirit of God who sustains us in the Christian life. But it is the Holy Spirit *working through the Word* who does this. It is not, as some seem to think, that the Holy Spirit brings life and power separately from God's Word, and only then is God's Word applied to keep us on the right tracks. No: life and power come *through* God's Word.

In order to understand this we need to do some careful thinking about what the Word of God is and what/who the Holy Spirit is. First of all, God's Word is not merely a book. It is God speaking to us. Primarily, God has spoken to us through a man, Jesus Christ. So, primarily, the Word of God is Jesus Christ. God has also spoken through his people, and continues to do so when they proclaim his Word in obedience to him. And God has spoken and does speak through the Bible.

Therefore, when I said above, 'the Holy Spirit works through the Word', I was not limiting God to a book. Rather, I am saying that there is something characteristic about the way the Holy Spirit operates. He is not merely a 'force for good in the world'. Nor does he perform blind acts of power which might achieve 'good things' but which have to be channelled by us in the correct direction. Yet it is apparent that the Holy Spirit is often regarded in this way by charismatics, and perhaps especially by some of those involved in the 'Toronto Blessing'. One distinctive feature of many 'Blessing'-type meetings has been the way the Holy Spirit is invoked by symbolic gestures. I am thinking of two gestures in particular. Those who have already 'received' often (instead of praying for the Holy Spirit to come on a person who is waiting to 'receive') use repeated waving gestures towards the person, as though they are pushing air or water in waves towards them. Another characteristic gesture has been one in which those who have already 'received' throw imaginary buckets of water over those 'receiving'. Quite often there is a corresponding physical reaction, even though there is no physical contact between those giving and those receiving. So, for example, somebody might 'throw' an imaginary bucket of water from several feet away and the person 'receiving' will respond immediately with a considerable increase of their physical phenomena, perhaps laughing louder and harder, or shaking more intensely. The significant thing about this is that, no matter what their theoretical beliefs are about the Holy Spirit, he is treated as a force (represented by air or water) at a person's command.

This tendency to treat the Holy Spirit as an impersonal force, available for Christians to control or 'dispense', has been a weakness of much Pentecostal and Charismatic

Christianity in this century. In terms of this section's title, it has been too infrequently recognised that the Holy Spirit is a 'who' not a 'what'. I hope that those involved in the 'Blessing' will redress their tendency to treat the Holy Spirit as an impersonal force with some good quality Trinitarian teaching. But such 'after-the-fact' teaching is far from ideal. It would be much better if the Holy Spirit were not treated as an impersonal force in the first place, available for Christians to 'dispense' as and when they wish.

The Holy Spirit is the Third Person of the Trinity, who acts where and as he wills. As the Third Person of the Trinity he works to bring human beings to a better understanding of their true position before God the Father and to a greater knowledge of God the Son. Some words of Jesus will illustrate what I mean:

> *'But when the Counsellor comes, whom I shall send to you from the Father, even the Spirit of truth, who proceeds from the Father, he will bear witness to me'* (Jn 15.26).

> *'Nevertheless I tell you the truth: it is to your advantage that I go away, for if I do not go away, the Counsellor will not come to you; but if I go, I will send him to you. And when he comes, he will convince the world concerning sin and righteousness and judgement'* (Jn 16.7-8).

> *'When the Spirit of truth comes, he will guide you into all the truth; for he will not speak on his own authority, but whatever he hears he will speak, and he will declare to you the things that are to come. He will glorify me, for he will take what is mine and declare it to you. All that the Father has is mine; therefore I said that he will take what is mine and declare it to you'* (Jn 16.13-15).

This is the work of the Holy Spirit. He is not an impersonal force performing blind acts of power. Rather, he brings human beings to a better understanding of their true position before God the Father and to a greater knowledge of God the Son. This is not to say that he does not cause miracles to happen. But it is to say that miracles from the Holy Spirit will bring people closer to God. To put it another way, when the Holy Spirit is at work, he draws us into eternal life by giving us knowledge of God: 'And this is eternal life, that they know thee the only true God, and Jesus Christ whom thou hast sent' (Jn 17.3).

Word and Spirit

Eternal life and knowledge of God come when we hear the gospel in faith (see Rom. 10.8-17). The next key point I want to raise, therefore, has to do with the fact that we are not born anew by the Spirit in an act that is separate from our hearing of the gospel. Rather, as the Word is proclaimed *to* us, the Spirit is at work *in* us. Nor does it stop there: as we go through our Christian lives hearing the Word proclaimed, the Holy Spirit works powerfully in us, transforming and sanctifying us. The Holy Spirit, in other words, works in us by the Word.

In much of the charismatic movement, however, that is not believed to be the case. Instead, the Holy Spirit and the Word are thought to operate separately. I discuss this in more detail in Chapter 5, but there is a false yet very influential division between experience and reason present in much of today's church. Experience is believed to be the realm of spirituality, the realm where the Holy Spirit is at work. The idea is summed up by the often-asked question, 'You believe it in your head, but do you know it in your heart?' It is also revealed in the following advice given to people attending a 'Blessing' meeting:

> *Relax:* God is unlikely to do something to you if you don't want it. However, often there is ambivalence within us. In our hearts we want more from God, but in our heads we don't. Thank God, he reads our heart and works in us anyway.'[7]

This kind of advice fails to take account of the fact that 'heart' in the Bible most often includes the intellect. In the Bible the 'heart' is commonly 'regarded as being the seat of the intellect, the feelings and the will'.[8] But that is little noticed, and the division between 'head' and 'heart' is accepted unquestioningly by many Christians. Once the division is accepted, it is the 'heart' which is believed to be important. As the quotation shows, the 'heart' is where true religion is supposed to be. The role of the 'head'—the role of reason—comes to be a secondary one: to ensure we do not do anything crazy, that we do not go off the rails. And this is where the Bible (and perhaps theology) enters the picture. Our understanding of the Bible is supposed to keep us from mad excesses. But on the other hand—so the argument goes—if we merely have the understanding then we will go nowhere at all. The truth alone, it is said, leads to dead orthodoxy.

All this results in a false understanding of how 'Word' and 'Spirit' are related to each other. It is thought that when the Word is predominant in a church (presumably through plenty of preaching and teaching), there will be an abundance of truth but very little power. On the other hand, where the Spirit predominates, there will be much power but also the danger of things going off the rails. Sometimes, the following rhyme is quoted to summarize this view:

> The Word without the Spirit, and you'll slow up.
>
> The Spirit without the Word, and you'll blow up.
>
> But Word and Spirit together, and you'll grow up.

Insofar as it provides a reminder that the Bible must not be discarded, the rhyme is to be welcomed. But notice how the first line implies that the Word can be had without the Spirit (leading to loss of vitality), while in the second line the Spirit can be had without the Word (leading to excess). It appears to teach that Word and Spirit ought to be held together only because then the Word will keep the life of the Spirit on the right track, not because the Spirit operates through the Word.

This is wrong. It is a misconception to think that the Holy Spirit moves with power separately from God's Word. I suspect that the misconception has arisen out of the extensive use, in Pentecostal and Charismatic circles, of the 'gifts of the Spirit', such as 'words of knowledge', 'prophecy', 'tongues' and so on. What we need to realise about these gifts is that they are exactly that: gifts. In a sense, God has given us control of them. Paul makes it clear (1 Cor. 14.26-32) that those who prophesy and speak in tongues, and presumably those who have the other gifts (of healing, wisdom, miracles, service etc.), are able to operate their gifts as they deem appropriate: 'the spirits of the prophets are subject to the prophets' (1 Cor. 14.32). These gifts can be, and sometimes are, operated in wrong contexts, with a wrong spirit and for wrong reasons. What is more, it is a notorious fact that churches where the gifts are in considerable use are susceptible to neglect of the Bible and preaching. This can, and does, give the false impression that powerful spiritual occurrences can be separated from the Word. It also gives the impression that the function of the Word is only to be a kind of safety-device or 'limiter' of power and life.

Charismatic gifts are not the Holy Spirit. God does *not* give us control of the Holy Spirit. For this reason, it is entirely possible for powerful and seemingly 'spiritual' things to happen, in which charismatic gifts are functioning impressively, without God's Holy Spirit being at work in a life-bringing manner. Some words of Jesus are salient here:

'Not every one who says to me, "Lord, Lord," shall enter the kingdom of heaven, but he who does the will of my Father who is in heaven. On that day many will say to me, "Lord, Lord, did we not prophesy in your name, and cast out demons in your name, and do many mighty works in your name?" And then will I declare to them, "I never knew you; depart from me, you evildoers."' (Mt. 7.21-23).

It would seem to be possible to operate charismatic gifts *against* the will of the Father, and to do so is to do evil. Pentecostals and charismatics need to face up to the uncomfortable fact that we often see manifestations of seemingly 'spiritual' power which God may well regard as evil because they are not directed as he wills.

That aside, the point I wish to make is that charismatic gifts can indeed be separated from the Word of God, and this has led people to the erroneous conclusion that the work of the Holy Spirit can be separated from the Word. We need to recognise that when God moved in power in the past it was because the gospel, his Word, was being proclaimed. Or perhaps we should put it the other way round: when the gospel was proclaimed with power in the past it was because God moved. Indeed, this seems to be the way Acts 2 explains things. On the day of Pentecost, the disciples 'were all filled with the Holy Spirit and began to speak in other tongues' (v. 4), and with these other tongues they declared 'the mighty works of God' (v. 11). When the Holy Spirit came in power, he caused the Word of God to be proclaimed to the world (Rom 15.18-19).

By contrast, in much of today's church the Spirit is divided from the Word. What is often not realised is that this kind of thinking is itself theology: bad theology. The dividing of reason from experience, head from heart, truth from life, and Word from Spirit, is theology; but it is not biblical. It is, as I shall demonstrate in Chapter 5, a modern reaction to the eighteenth-century Enlightenment. In my view, this bad theology has had a very significant effect upon the way the 'Toronto Blessing' has come into the church.

Conclusion

In Jesus' teaching, word, spirit, truth and life are bound up together, and have their unity in him:

> *'Truly, truly, I say to you, he who hears my word and believes him who sent me, has eternal life; he does not come into judgement, but has passed from death to life'* (Jn 5.24).

> *'It is the spirit that gives life, the flesh is of no avail; the words that I have spoken to you are spirit and life'* (Jn 6.63).

> *Simon Peter answered him, 'Lord, to whom shall we go? You have the words of eternal life'* (Jn 6.68).

> *'I am the way, and the truth, and the life; no one comes to the Father, but by me'* (Jn 14.6).

Jesus also taught that, when he left the earth, the Holy Spirit would come to enable us to enter into truth and so into life:

> *'When the Spirit of truth comes, he will guide you into all the truth'* (Jn 16.13).

These verses make it clear that our minds are crucial to our faith, since it is by our minds that we understand Jesus' words of truth and so enter into eternal life. Our thinking should not be regarded as secondary. We must resist the idea that the Holy Spirit works in our hearts and not our minds, that 'experience' is the realm of true spirituality and that reason tends to get in the way; or even the idea that reason is useful but only insofar as it provides a necessary control on our spirituality.

We must resist any division between Spirit and Word, even a division which is supposed to be overcome by holding the two separate things together. Instead, we must maintain the truth that the Holy Spirit works through the Word. If we remember the that Jesus Christ, as the Word of God, is God's communication to us in and through the Holy Spirit, then Trinitarian theology will help us: Jesus Christ, the Word of God, at the behest of the Father, is at work in the World through the Holy Spirit.

NOTES
1. See his article '"Toronto" and Scripture', in *Renewal magazine* (No. 222; November, 1994), pp. 24-27, here p. 24.
2. See M. Fearon, *A Breath of Fresh Air* (Guildford: Eagle, 1994), p. 94.
3. See Chevreau, *Catch the Fire* (London: Marshall Pickering, 1994), p. 22.
4. Ibid, p. 24.
5. Ibid, p. 53.
6. '"Toronto" and Scripture', p. 24.
7. P. Nodding, 'The Holy Spirit in our midst', in W. Boulton (ed.), *The Impact of Toronto* (Crowborough: Monarch, 1995), p. 35.
8. *The Zondervan Pictorial Bible Dictionary* (Grand Rapids, MI: Zondervan, 3rd edn, 1967), p. 340.

CHAPTER 4

What about the Fruit?

We have seen that there are serious problems with describing the 'Toronto Blessing' as 'biblical', or as 'non-biblical but approved by God. We turn now to consider the most important part of the whole debate. This is the argument that the fruit of the 'Blessing' proves it is of God—that we should be convinced by the good which is being produced. 'I am so glad', says Terry Virgo, leader of the New Frontiers International group of churches, 'that, from the beginning, I saw substantial spiritual fruit in the lives of those affected. The immediate manifestations were so strange, but the continuing impact on people's lives has been magnificent.'[1] Advocates of the 'Blessing' believe that, even if all else fails, on this score they are following a biblical path: the Bible teaches that we must look to the fruit of a tree in order to know if its roots are good.

Put like that, the issue seems fairly 'cut and dried'; but, as we will see, there are a number of strands to the fruit argument which need to be unravelled. Each section of this chapter deals with one strand, and asks whether advocates of the 'Blessing' really are as close to biblical teaching as they think. The first strand is summarized by the phrase 'testing the spirits'.

Testing the Spirits

Guy Chevreau, in *Catch the Fire*, his apologetic for the 'Blessing', asserts that the question of fruit is much more important than doubts about the strange physical phenomena. He puts it this way:

> A curious manifestation has been exhibited at the Airport meetings, and noted elsewhere. Those affected jump up and down in one spot, sometimes for extended periods of time. Not surprisingly, the phenomenon has been dubbed 'pogoing'. To my knowledge there is no Biblical parallel, or basis for such a manifestation of the Spirit's power and presence on a person. Does that mean that it is necessarily 'of the flesh'? Should pogo-ers be taken aside immediately, and corrected?
>
> Such a commitment to rigid biblical literalism is not conducive to the Spirit of revival. Suffice it to say that there is little by way of a biblical basis to 'prove' the validity of ANY particular manifestation. There is, however, clear counsel to 'test the spirits' (1 John 4:1ff). That test lies, not so much on what is happening physically, on the outside of the pogo-er, but spiritually, on the 'inside'. One of the key tests is a simple, but subjective one: having bounced, or better, been bounced, does the person love Jesus more?[2]

It is clear from the second part of this quotation that Chevreau sees the counsel in 1 John to 'test the spirits' as advice to consider the results (or fruit) of the experience. The test has two stages. First, the person is asked to give his or her testimony as to what has happened inside them as a result of the experience. Those hearing the testimony must subjectively judge whether what has happened amounts to the person 'loving Jesus more' (or to them having attained some other spiritual virtue in greater measure). The second stage of the test—not mentioned by Chevreau—requires time. People must judge whether the effect of the experience is lasting. This is because true fruit of the Spirit remains and does not fade away.

Anyone who reads or hears arguments in favour of the 'Toronto Blessing' will know that the first stage of this 'simple, but subjective' test has come to be of paramount importance, and has carried the day with many. In the face of testimonies provided by people who have just returned from Toronto, or from a Toronto-type meeting, large numbers of churches and Christians have felt compelled to accept that the 'Blessing' is of God, and to welcome it among them, despite the bizarre phenomena involved. Testimonies about the fruit of the 'Blessing' are pivotal to the belief that it is a movement which has been instigated and sustained by the Spirit of God.

I will return to the question of how we are to judge the individual testimonies later. What I want to do here is consider whether the procedure of proving the 'Blessing' by means of testimonies measures up to the biblical concept of 'testing the spirits'. Supporters of the 'Blessing' clearly think that it does. Chevreau justifies his position by quoting the phrase 'test the spirits' from 1 Jn 4.1, but is he right to do so? We need to look carefully at the passage the phrase comes from. 1 Jn 4.1-6 runs as follows:

> *Beloved, do not believe every spirit, but test the spirits to see whether they are of God; for many false prophets have gone out into the world. By this you know the Spirit of God: every spirit which confesses that Jesus Christ has come in the flesh is of God, and every spirit which does not confess Jesus is not of God. This is the spirit of antichrist, of which you heard that it was coming, and now it is in the world already. Little children, you are of God, and have overcome them; for he who is in you is*

*greater than he who is in the world. They are of the world,
therefore what they say is of the world, and the world listens to
them. We are of God. Whoever knows God listens to us, and he
who is not of God does not listen to us. By this we know the
spirit of truth and the spirit of error.*

We need to ask two questions. First, what does John
intend his test to be applied to? Secondly, how is the test to
be carried out? When we have answers to these, we will be
close to knowing whether the passage tells us to follow the
kind of procedure for testing that proponents of the 'Blessing'
recommend.

We can begin by considering why John says, 'Do not
believe every spirit'. It appears that in the community of
believers to which John addresses his letter, as elsewhere in
the early church (for example, in Corinth), considerable
prestige was being given to those who spoke in tongues and
prophesied. This raised the problem of how genuinely Spirit-
inspired activity could be distinguished from falsely-inspired
activity. The problem was particularly acute because people
had come among the believers seeking to deceive them (see 1
Jn 2.26). These people sought to gain a hearing by speaking in
tongues and prophesying. In response, John warns the
community 'not to believe every spirit'.

This gives us an initial answer to our first question:
John intends the test to be applied to people who claim to
exhibit manifestations of the Holy Spirit, and who, on the
strength of that, are deceiving believers with 'anti-Christian'
teaching. (They are 'antichrists'—see 1 Jn 2.18-23.)

Having established this, it is important to make clear
what John means by 'spirits'. Sometimes, readers think he is
talking about evil beings which possess people and prevent
them from confessing Jesus. In that case, 'testing the spirits'

would involve discovering whether something has happened because of the influence of a demon. This is not what John means, as we can see from the way he uses the phrase 'every spirit' in verse 2, 'every spirit which confesses that Jesus Christ has come in the flesh is of God'. This cannot be referring to demonic forces, so it must be that John is speaking of human spirits. Some people, because the Holy Spirit has made their spirits to be spirits of truth, confess the truth that Jesus Christ has come in the flesh. There are other people, though, who are in error and are unable to recognise the truth (v. 3). This is not because they are possessed by demons, but because their own spirit has not been made anew by the Holy Spirit.

Now to our second question, how is the test to be carried out? Or, put differently, what does 'testing the spirits' involve?

John says, 'By this you know the Spirit of God: every spirit which confesses that Jesus Christ has come in the flesh is of God, and every spirit which does not confess Jesus is not of God.' These words tell us that those who were causing trouble in the community held heretical beliefs about Jesus' nature. It is impossible to be exact about the details of these beliefs, but it is likely that on the one hand some believed that Jesus was only human and not divine—that he was not the Son of God (see 2.23)—and on the other hand some believed that he was only divine and not human—that he had not 'come in the flesh'. John suggests a confession which will bring such heresies to light: someone who believes that Jesus was not human will not confess that Jesus came in the flesh.

Of course, by 'confession' John does not mean mere recitation of the words, 'Jesus Christ has come in the flesh'. A person must truly believe what they confess. As we will see in

Chapter 5, belief cannot be confined to an artificially-detached intellectual realm. Rather, belief affects our whole being and all our actions. True belief issues in right action. This is why running all through 1 John are statements like, 'If we say we have fellowship with him while we walk in darkness, we lie and do not live according to the truth' (1.6); and, 'He who says "I know him" but disobeys his commandments is a liar, and the truth is not in him' (2.4). We can conclude, therefore, that the test to see whether a person's spirit is of God involves assessment of whether that person declares true belief and lives accordingly.

(I have generalised from the specific confession which John gives and have said 'true belief', because the confession of 1 John 4 was tailored to the specific situation John was writing to. In a different situation, with different heresies present, a different confession would be appropriate. The important point to realise is that true or right belief is a crucial element of the test.)

With this established, we can return to the question of how the procedure recommended by 'Blessing' supporters measures up.

The first conclusion I reached about the injunction to 'test the spirits' was that John intends the test to be applied to people who claim to exhibit manifestations of the Holy Spirit. Therefore, since people involved in the 'Toronto Blessing' claim to do just that, it is appropriate to apply the test to them. However, we need to add an extremely important proviso: the test cannot prove (or disprove) that the physical phenomena of the 'Blessing' are 'of God'. It can only help decide whether a particular person is 'of God' or not. The test is intended to tell us about a person who is 'manifesting', not about their 'manifestations'. John and those he is writing to already know that such things as prophecy and speaking in tongues are of God, and that these things also have counterfeits. What the test is designed to do is help them decide who among the ones 'manifesting' are real Christians, and who are not and must not be given a hearing.

I believe that people who are arguing in support of the 'Blessing' have got this confused. They treat the test as a means of deciding whether the strange phenomena are of God, when the test is not designed to answer that question. A prime example of such confusion is found in Mark Stibbe's book, *Times of Refreshing*. Stibbe realises that 'Christians are as vulnerable to deception as non-Christians',[3] so he sets out what he thinks is a 'Biblical theology of discernment' in a section entitled 'Criteria for Testing'.[4] I will return to his 'criteria for testing' in a moment, but first we need to look at what he says in the subsequent section of *Times of Refreshing*, pp. 39-44. entitled 'Testing the Spirits'. This title indicates his intention to follow the kind of procedure found in 1 John 4.

He begins by saying,

> Having provided a Biblical theology of discernment we are now in a position to return to the subject of the Toronto blessing and ask, 'Is this a work of the Holy Spirit or not?'[5]

Next comes *the* crucial part of his book. Stibbe offers to his readers, as proof of the divine nature of the 'Toronto Blessing', the testimony of a member of his own church who had been to Toronto. In the testimony she recounts what happened to her there, and its effects. It is certainly a beautiful and moving testimony. Stibbe says of it,

> The whole experience is emphatically Christ-centred. In fact, if you read carefully, you will see that

> it is thoroughly Trinitarian: a new sense of the healing
> love of God the Father, the saving grace of God the
> Son, and the awesome power of God the Holy Spirit.
> What could be more Christian than that?[6]

There is no need to reproduce the testimony here. Having read it, I see little reason to disagree with Stibbe's assessment. What I do disagree with, however, is the use he makes of the testimony. He argues that, having applied his method of discernment to it, we must conclude,

> that this is the Lord's work, and it is marvellous in
> our eyes! The fact that this story is representative of
> the vast majority of a huge and growing number of
> testimonies means that *we are left with no alternative
> but to say that the Toronto blessing is indeed the
> Lord's work* ... [T]he truth of the matter is that *such
> testimonies are signs of a major new work of the Holy
> Spirit of God.* [7]

I have italicised the key phrases. They assert that testimonies about 'Blessing' experiences and their fruit prove that the movement has been instigated and sustained by the Spirit of God. As I have shown, this is not what 'testing the spirits' is about in 1 John 4. The test is neither about religious movements nor strange phenomena. It is about whether certain people who are apparently displaying manifestations of the Spirit, and who on that basis are seeking a place of influence in the Christian community, should be allowed to do what they want.

Confusion about what the test of 1 John 4 is designed to do is displayed by an oft-added qualification about the need to allow time to pass. Stibbe says, 'the blessing must be allowed to take root and bear fruit before we can properly assess its authenticity and holiness'. On this view, the test enables us to make a tentative, initial judgement about whether the movement is of God, a judgement which can be reassessed as time passes. According to 1 John 4, however, the test enables us to make a definite, immediate judgement about people, people who, if they are not of God, should be rejected by the community. In the community to which John writes, heretics are causing trouble. As 1 Jn 2.18-22 puts it, they have the spirit of antichrist. Their presence must therefore be discerned immediately and their influence removed. This is what 'testing the spirits' is for; it is not intended to discern whether certain experiences, or certain religious movements, are of God.

In summary: advocates of the 'Toronto Blessing' have misunderstood 'testing the spirits' in two ways. They have misunderstood both the nature of the test and what it is supposed to do. First, advocates of the 'Blessing' think that the test involves testimony about what an experience has done for a person when it actually involves confession of what a person believes. Second, they think that it tells us about the nature of experiences when it actually tells us about the nature of people (i.e. whether they are Christians or not). In Chapter 6, I will explain how a properly-understood 'testing of the spirits' ought to be applied in the context of the 'Toronto Blessing'.

Discerning the Spirits

At this point, it will be valuable to consider Paul's phrase, 'discerning of spirits' (1 Cor. 12.10). This phrase sounds as if it ought to be applicable in some way to spiritual experiences. Certainly, the call for 'discernment' can be heard on all sides of the debate.

As far as I can tell, there are two distinct understandings of how 'discerning of spirits' works. Normally the word 'discernment' is used to denote the need to think carefully about spiritual matters and to make informed, well-balanced judgements about them. On this understanding, people who have the gift of discerning of spirits have particularly good critical faculties with regard to spiritual matters. They are able to assess what they see happening and decide whether there are signs that it may not be from God.

Others understand the gift rather differently. It is not a question of certain people having particularly good critical faculties. Rather, certain people, regardless of their critical abilities, are able to hear directly from God whether a particular occurrence is caused by the Holy Spirit or by some other spiritual force. It is implied by some advocates of the 'Toronto Blessing' that people who have the gift of discernment have already 'discerned' that the 'Blessing' is a movement from God. In addition, it seems to be believed that leaders of 'Blessing'-type meetings, at necessary moments, by this gift of the Holy Spirit, are enabled to discern which among the strange phenomena are from the Spirit and which are counterfeit, even though to all other onlookers one manifestation may look much like another.[8] Clearly, we need to ascertain whether the gift of discernment should be understood in this way.

Unfortunately, the gift is not explained in any detail by Paul, so it is difficult to be sure exactly what he meant. We can, however, get some idea. The passage in which the phrase is found is 1 Cor. 12.7-10:

> *To each is given the manifestation of the Spirit for the common good. To one is given through the Spirit the utterance of wisdom, and to another the utterance of knowledge according*

to the same Spirit, to another faith by the same Spirit, to another gifts of healing by the one Spirit, to another the working of miracles, to another prophecy, to another the ability to distinguish between spirits, to another various kinds of tongues, to another the interpretation of tongues.

The latter part of the passage is intended by Paul to illustrate his opening statement, that a variety of spiritual gifts are given to Christians for the common good. By listing nine different such gifts, one of which is the ability to distinguish between (or discern) spirits, he emphasizes that variety. He knows that the Corinthians are familiar with these gifts, so he feels no need to describe what they are for and how they work. Consequently, we cannot be certain from the passage what the gift of distinguishing between spirits means.

Fortunately, there are a number of points which can help us. First, the Greek word for 'distinguish' (*diakrisis*) also appears in 1 Cor. 14.29, where Paul talks about the need for discerning, differentiating or properly judging prophecies. Second, in 1 Thess. 5.20-21 Paul tells the Thessalonian Christians that they should 'not despise prophecies, but test everything'. That is, they should continue to exercise the gift of prophecy rather than let it be replaced by other things, but they should not allow the pendulum to swing too far the other way and naïvely accept everything that is said under the guise of 'prophecy'. Instead, every prophecy must be carefully tested.[9]

These two points suggest that when Paul mentions 'discerning of spirits' in 1 Cor. 12.10 he may be thinking of the gift as operating primarily in the area of judgement of prophecies. As Gordon Fee points out, this is made all the more likely by the fact that Paul lists the gift immediately after the gift of prophecy in 1 Cor. 12.10.[10] In addition, the next two gifts in the list are 'tongues' and 'interpretation of tongues'. Fee points out that, 'This same pattern of tongues plus interpretation and prophecy plus discernment is found again in 14.26-29.'[11]

We saw earlier that in 1 John 4 the phrase 'test the spirits' has to do with whether a person confesses truth or error. It seems likely that Paul means something similar by 'distinguishing between spirits', but this time with respect to prophecy, not confession. The ability to distinguish between spirits is the ability to tell whether a person is prophesying truth out of a truthful spirit (which, of course, the Holy Spirit creates in us) or error out of a false spirit. Thus Fee concludes regarding the gift,

> in this present listing, it seems most likely that Paul is referring to the same phenomenon as in 14:29 [namely, weighing what the prophets say], but is using the language of 'spirits' to refer to the prophetic utterances that need to be 'differentiated' by the others in the community who also have the Spirit and so can discern what is truly of the Spirit.[12]

Hence, while the 1 John 4 test is intended to answer the question of whether certain people should be barred from any influence in the Christian community, the gift of discernment is something that is to be applied to all prophetic utterances given by members of the community. Those who are welcomed as members of the community must expect that what they say prophetically will be tested by those who are discerning. In contrast to 1 John 4, the issue is not whether certain people are 'of God', but whether certain prophecies are 'of God'.

The details of how 'distinguishing between spirits' ought to operate would have to be considered in a book on prophecy, not in a book on the 'Toronto Blessing'. The key point here is that it is not a gift which offers a kind of spiritual litmus test for anything supposedly spiritual that happens in the Christian community. Rather, it concerns true and false prophecy. It has to do with whether what people say 'in the name of the Lord' really is from God. It should not, therefore, be assumed that the ability to discern between spirits will enable Christians to say that the 'Blessing' as a whole or its individual phenomena are of God or not of God. The issue cannot be decided in that way.

Testing the Fruit

This does not mean that we should not try to discern the truth about the 'Toronto Blessing'. It means only that the presence of the gift of discernment in Christian communities does not provide a kind of automatic immunity from error. It cannot be taken for granted that those who are gifted in discernment will be able to tell whether the 'Blessing' is of God or not. Instead, we must set about the difficult task of assessing the 'Blessing' according to biblical criteria. It is appropriate now to return to Mark Stibbe's 'biblical theology of discernment'. He defends the 'Blessing' by offering three 'biblical criteria for discernment'[13]: 'christology', 'character' and 'consequence'.

The Test of Christology

Therefore I want you to understand that no one speaking by the Spirit of God ever says 'Jesus be cursed!' and no one can say 'Jesus is Lord' except by the Holy Spirit (1 Cor. 12.3).

Stibbe bases his 'test of Christology' on this text. He says, 'If a spiritual manifestation is motivated by the Holy Spirit, then we can be sure that it will result in Jesus of Nazareth being exalted as Lord.'[14] We need to ask whether this is a correct understanding of the text.

The situation at Corinth appears to display both similarities and differences to the one addressed in 1 John 4. The main similarity appears to be that members of both communities tended to assign considerable prestige to those who were exhibiting supposed manifestations of the Spirit. In Corinth, they were setting great store by the gift of tongues: those who spoke most in tongues were taken to be the most 'spiritual'. The main difference appears to be that Paul is not dealing with the problem of people deceiving the community with heretical views (though there may be an element of this), rather, he is addressing the question of the significance of spiritual gifts, especially tongues.

The Greek of 1 Cor. 12.2 (the verse preceding our text), is difficult to translate. But Gordon Fee, in his commentary on 1 Corinthians, offers a convincing rendition: 'When you were pagans, you were carried away, as you were continually being led about to mute idols.' He then comments,

> In keeping with his Jewish heritage, Paul scorns the idols as mute because they cannot hear and answer prayer; nor can they speak—in contrast to the Spirit of God who can. But he has also argued earlier that the mute idols represent demons (10:20-21)—who can speak and do speak through their devotees. Most likely, therefore, he is reminding them of what they well know, that in some of the cults 'inspired utterances' were part of the worship, despite the 'mute idols.'[15]

On this basis, Fee concludes that Paul's intention in 1 Cor. 12.2-3 is to establish,

> that it is not 'inspired speech' as such that is evidence of the Spirit. They had already known that phenomenon as pagans. Rather, what counts is the *intelligible and Christian content* of such utterances.[16]

After all, it is possible for somebody, under the guise of 'inspiration', to say something blasphemous. This is why Paul says in verse 3, 'I want you to understand that no one speaking by the Spirit of God ever says "Jesus be cursed!" and no one can say "Jesus is Lord" except by the Holy Spirit'. Verse 3, therefore, is not intended to be a test. Rather, it is an admonition that 'manifestations' are not in themselves proof of the Spirit's presence, and a reminder that the Holy Spirit will always lead Christians to exalt Jesus as Lord.[17]

It is right to say that we can be sure the Spirit is at work in a person if they truly are exalting Jesus Christ. But as with 1 John 4 Stibbe again confuses matters. He thinks that a 'test of christology' can tell us about the value of certain experiences. It cannot. Rather, it indicates whether the Spirit is at work in a person. Paul did not write 1 Cor. 12.3 to give the Corinthians a way of deciding whether the phenomenon of speaking in tongues is of God—they already knew that in some cases it is and in some cases it is not. Rather, he wrote it to remind them that truly spiritual Christians are those who confess the Lordship of Jesus—regardless of how much they speak in tongues.

The proper way to apply the test in the context of the 'Toronto Blessing' would be to ask whether the testimony in question exalts Jesus as Lord and, more generally, whether it declares other truths about God. If it does (and given that the person testifying lives a life in accordance with these truths), then we can say that the person testifying is a spiritual person, a person in whom the Holy Spirit is active. It seems to me that the testimony which Stibbe uses does indeed have these characteristics. Yet that tells us only that the woman testifying is spiritual. It does not tell us that the 'Blessing' is of God. Furthermore, the fact that there are, in Stibbe's words, 'a huge and growing number of testimonies' like this one tells us only that a large number of good Christians are involved. It does not leave us 'with no alternative but to say that the Toronto blessing is indeed the Lord's work'.[18]

The Test of Character

Mark Stibbe says, 'When a spiritual manifestation promotes a radical and active love of God and for others, then that experience is to be welcomed. That, in brief, is the test of character.'[19] In other words, the 'Blessing' improves the Christian character of those who get involved with it. In particular, it increases a person's Christ-like love. Because it does this, the 'Blessing' passes the 'test of character'. This test that is regularly found in discussions of the 'Toronto Blessing'. Guy Chevreau's version has already been cited: 'One of the key tests is a simple, but subjective one: having bounced, or better, been bounced, does the person love Jesus more?'[20]

We need not spend as long on this, because advocates of the 'Toronto Blessing' make the same mistake with it as they do with the test of Christology. They think it can be applied to supposed 'manifestations of the Spirit' such as are found in the 'Toronto Blessing' when in fact it can only be applied to people. It is surprising that Stibbe makes this mistake, because at one point he actually states rightly how it is to work. Commenting on 1 Jn 3.23, he says,

> John, we should note, has several fundamental criteria for helping his congregations to be sure that they are Christians. The first is whether or not they believe that Jesus is the Son of God. The second is whether or not they love the brethren. If they do both, they can be certain that they belong to God ... The

second is important when we consider the test of character.[21]

Stibbe here correctly states that the test helps us to know who is a Christian. But later he wrongly claims that the New Testament teaching is that the test of character helps us know that a spiritual manifestation is of God.

His argument runs as follows:

> Paul's teaching in I Corinthians 12–14 is unavoidably clear: if a charismatic experience is truly inspired by God, then love will be the chief quality visible in the character of the recipient. When a spiritual manifestation promotes a radical and active love of God and for others, then that experience is to be welcomed. That, in brief, is the test of character.[22]

This argument is based on the erroneous assumption that Paul believes that 'spiritual manifestation' can increase love in the person having the experience. In fact, Paul teaches that true Christian love is a different thing from spiritual manifestations, and it is something Christians should strive for above any desire for gifts of the Spirit or 'manifestations'. He does not advise the Corinthians to have more manifestations so that their love will be increased. Indeed, as we have seen, they were having too many 'spiritual experiences', especially speaking in tongues, and were greatly lacking in love.

It is not wrong to seek the gifts. But, says Paul,

> *I will show you a still more excellent way. If I speak in the tongues of men and of angels, but have not love, I am a noisy gong or a clanging cymbal. And if I have prophetic powers, and understand all mysteries and all knowledge, and if I have all faith, so as to remove mountains, but have not love, I am nothing. If I give away all I have, and if I deliver my body to be burned, but have not love, I gain nothing. Love is patient and kind; love is not jealous or boastful; it is not arrogant or rude. Love does not insist on its own way; it is not irritable or*

resentful; it does not rejoice at wrong, but rejoices in the right. Love bears all things, believes all things, hopes all things, endures all things. Love never ends; as for prophecies, they will pass away; as for tongues, they will cease; as for knowledge, it will pass away. For our knowledge is imperfect and our prophecy is imperfect; but when the perfect comes, the imperfect will pass away. When I was a child, I spoke like a child, I thought like a child, I reasoned like a child; when I became a man, I gave up childish ways. For now we see in a mirror dimly, but then face to face. Now I know in part; then I shall understand fully, even as I have been fully understood. So faith, hope, love abide, these three; but the greatest of these is love.

(1 Cor. 12.31b–13.13)

There is no suggestion here that charismatic experience enables us to love better. Paul is surely teaching that love is a different and much greater thing than any spiritual gift or manifestation.

Love for the Christian is a matter of the will, a matter of us choosing to be patient and kind, a matter of us rejecting the sinful urges to jealousy or boasting, and so on. That is why Paul says, 'Make love your aim' (1 Cor 14.1a), and only then says 'and earnestly desire the spiritual gifts' (14.1b). He does not say, 'Earnestly desire the spiritual gifts so that your love will be increased'. According to Paul, the spiritual gifts are for edification (14.4), not for miraculously enabling us to love more. His teaching in 1 Corinthians 12–14 is clear: when a spiritual gift is operated in love, then the operation of that gift is to be welcomed, but otherwise it is worthless.

Everything that Christians do, including exhibiting manifestations of the Spirit, should be done in love for God and others. This is a requirement of all Christians. All Christians are commanded to 'make love your aim'. Or, in the words of 1 Jn 3.23, we are to 'love one another, just as he has commanded us'. It is an area in which we all fail. It is the hardest part of the Christian life. But it is not an area in which certain of us (perhaps those involved in the 'Toronto Blessing') are given a special enabling by means of unusual spiritual experiences.

When put this way, it is clear that the 'test of character' can no longer act as proof for whether or not the experiences and 'manifestations' of the 'Toronto Blessing' are of God. All it can do is show whether or not the people involved are living as God commands them to live.

In fact, to many observers it does *not* seem that the 'Toronto Blessing' is leading to a great number of Christians giving themselves in self-sacrificial love to the service of God and others. Rather, it seems that the 'Blessing' causes some to seek after their own needs above those of others. There are many reports of Christians returning night after night to Toronto-type meetings to get more of the experience. It is possible that things may change, but at the time of writing the 'Blessing' has the characteristics of a movement which turns the church in on itself, not outwards in service of others.

Finally regarding the 'test of character', it is important to remember that it should be just that, a test of *character*. The test of whether somebody loves more is a test of what they do, not of what they say. When people testify to having greater feelings of love as a result of their experiences, that has little evidential value. It is well known that 'good experiences', whether they are induced by alcohol, drugs or even listening to beautiful music, can make people *feel* more loving. But once the effects of the experience wear off so do the feelings. The question then is, what does the person *do*?

The Test of Consequence

The third and final test in Mark Stibbe's 'biblical theology of discernment' is what he calls the 'test of consequence'. It involves the claim that the 'Blessing' experience leads a person to display, for example, an *increased* love of Jesus. It changes the person in a 'Godward' direction. Such a change, it is argued, must have been caused by the Holy Spirit.

For the purposes of clarity, it is important to treat this test separately, even though it is usually combined with the other two. Chevreau, for example, combines the test of character (the requirement to love) with this one when he asks, 'having bounced ... does the person love Jesus *more*?' Stibbe combines the test of Christology with this one when he asks, is the recipient '*moved to a greater level* of awareness of the reality, the nature and the Lordship of Jesus Christ?'[23]

I have italicised the words which emphasise that it is the claim that the 'Toronto Blessing' brings change which is key. For many, this is the clinching argument. On the basis of testimonies, they are convinced that the 'Blessing' really is changing people for the better, it really is bearing fruit. 'Fruit' is the crucial word here, because it is a biblical concept, and so people believe that in 'looking for the fruit' they are being biblical.

In a moment we will consider what the Bible teaches, but first I want to highlight the fact that, at least in the early days of the 'Toronto Blessing', while 'the fruit' was often the clinching argument, not enough time had actually passed for anyone to properly judge what 'the fruit' was and whether it was lasting. This led to the irony that, on the one hand, proponents pointed to the supposed fruit while, on the other hand, critics were 'counselled' to 'wait and see'. Which is it to be? If fruit shows its nature only after some time, then it seems to me that it was wrong for proponents of the 'Blessing' in the early days of the movement to make 'the fruit' a pivotal argument.

Be that as it may, let us now look at what the Bible teaches about 'fruit'. The text Stibbe uses is Mt. 7.15-20:

> *Beware of false prophets, who come to you in sheep's clothing but inwardly are ravenous wolves. You will know them by their fruits. Are grapes gathered from thorns, or figs from thistles? So, every sound tree bears good fruit, but the bad tree bears evil fruit. A sound tree cannot bear evil fruit, nor can a bad tree bear good fruit. Every tree that does not bear good fruit is cut down and thrown into the fire. Thus you will know them by their fruits.*

Stibbe rightly notes that Jesus warned that 'People with a deceptively authoritative charisma would emerge in [the first] churches. They were to be watched and assessed.' He then asks, 'How were they to be evaluated?' His answer is crucial: they were to be evaluated 'by the consequences of their ministry.'[24] By this he means that we should ask whether their ministry helps to 'heal relationships, strengthen unity, build up the body of Christ', and so on.[25]

Is that what Jesus means? Does Jesus teach the disciples to recognise false prophets *by the consequences of their ministry*? If so, he is teaching that they must be allowed quite some time to develop their ministries in churches, that they must be allowed considerable influence in the body of Christ. This seems unlikely to me. Can it be that Jesus wants people who are inwardly like 'ravenous wolves' to be allowed their freedom in the flock of God? If such a procedure were correct, then inevitably a large number of Christians and their churches will have to lead blighted lives for a considerable time. We must also consider whether such Christians, having been deceived for an extended period, would then be able to make a judgement about the ministry of their leaders.

In fact, Jesus teaches something rather different. There are two other occasions in Matthew's Gospel when the imagery of trees and fruit occurs. The first is John the Baptist's admonition to the Pharisees and Sadducees who came to him for baptism: 'Bear fruit that befits repentance ... Even now the axe is laid to the root of the trees; every tree therefore that does not bear good fruit is cut down and thrown into the fire' (Mt. 3.8-10). In this case, it is clear that the 'fruit' is the deeds and character which ought to follow the repentance of an individual.

Passing over Mt. 7.15-20 for the moment, the next occurrence is in Mt. 12.33. This verse follows the terrible accusation from some Pharisees that Jesus was casting out demons by the power of Beelzebul. Jesus replies, 'Either make the tree good, and its fruit good; or make the tree bad, and its fruit bad; for the tree is known by its fruit. You brood of vipers! How can you speak good, when you are evil? For out of the abundance of the heart the mouth speaks.' Here Jesus teaches that evil words such as came from these Pharisees are the result of evil hearts. The imagery of tree and its fruit is used to illustrate this.

In Mt. 3.8-10 and 12.33, then, the 'tree' stands for a person and the 'fruit' stands for that person's deeds, words and character. If we now reconsider Mt. 7.15-20, it becomes clear that we are not to evaluate possible 'false prophets' by the consequences of their church ministries as assessed over time. It is not a question, as it were, of their public ministry. Rather, it is a question of their character. We are to ask, what do they say and what do they do? This will include their behaviour and words both in public and in private. It will include their theological pronouncements (compare the Pharisees' words in Mt. 12.24) as well as the way they talk about ordinary matters.

These are judgements that can be made relatively early on when new people come into churches seeking leadership roles. As we get to know them, and before we allow them into positions of influence, we will be able to see their deeds, hear their words, and so discern their character. By their fruit we will judge whether they are good or bad. If they are bad, we will be wise not to allow them among us, for according to Jesus, they are 'ravenous wolves'.

Jesus' very next words are instructive on this. We had occasion to consider them in the previous chapter, and they are important again here:

> *'Not every one who says to me, "Lord, Lord," shall enter the kingdom of heaven, but he who does the will of my Father who is in heaven. On that day many will say to me, "Lord, Lord, did we not prophesy in your name, and cast out demons in your name, and do many mighty works in your name?" And then will I declare to them, "I never knew you; depart from me, you evildoers"' (Mt. 7.21-23).*

It sounds very much like Jesus is talking here about people who make claims for themselves on the basis of their public ministry. People who prophesy, cast out demons and do mighty works, all in Jesus' name, may well think of themselves as having produced wonderful 'fruit'. And the people around them may judge the same. But in Jesus' eyes, some of them are evildoers. Jesus teaches us to look at the 'fruit' in the sense of character, words and deeds, not in the sense of spiritual manifestations and ministries.

Stibbe has derived his 'test of consequence' from Mt. 7.15-20 wrongly. The test should be a test of the character of potential leaders not of their ministry results. In Chapter 6, I will describe how I think the test should be applied to the 'Toronto Blessing'. However, we need here to analyse the substance of Stibbe's test of consequence, since—whether or not it can be derived from Matthew 7—it does sound useful. He describes it as follows:

> The church is like a spiritual temple. It is being built up on the earth as the years go by. Everything which results in the church being built up can be regarded as inspired by the Holy Spirit. If such things heal relationships, strengthen unity, build up the body of Christ, then they are of God. That, in brief, is the test of consequence.[26]

I think that most Christians will agree with Stibbe's premise, that whatever builds up the church is inspired by God's Spirit. However, we need to assess how far this truth can be treated as a test. For here are a number of difficulties.

Church history shows that at times the Holy Spirit may cause things to happen which to human eyes appear to operate in the 'wrong' direction. In the sixteenth-century Reformation the Holy Spirit did a mighty work in the church: among other things, he restored the principle that we are justified by faith alone to its rightful place. But to human eyes it appeared that Martin Luther was causing great division by his insistence on the principle of justification by faith. He took a stance which led to a terrible splintering of the church. If 'building up the church' had been made the decisive test *at the time*, the Reformation would not have happened.

Conversely, Christians judge that, at times, things which some people have thought good for the church—which will 'build it up'—have in fact harmed the church. For example, attempts at church unification earlier this century, have been criticised for compromising important truths. Unity is extremely important, of course. It is something all

Christians should strive for. Naturally, it should never be sacrificed for the sake of petty theological preferences, minor differences of opinion and the like. Many divisions have been caused by people proudly holding on to their own preferences when there was no real need. But this does not alter the fact that, on occasions, the appearance of unity among Christians may have to be sacrificed for the sake of the cause of Christ.

To be fair to Stibbe, I imagine he is thinking more of the 'building up' that takes place in local church situations, of the changes that take place at the level of personal relationships. He is right that at this level some positive things have happened. There are people who, having previously had differences with others, have decided that these should be put aside in the light of what they see to be an amazing move of God. They have come to see such things as insignificant. In and of itself, this is undoubtedly good.

But can this be treated as a test? Does the fact that people put aside petty differences in the face of a great cause prove the rightness of that cause? It does not. At the beginning of the Second World War the German people united for their war effort just as much as the British people did. Similarly, to return to the Reformation, Christian people united in opposition to Luther just as much as other Christians united in support of him. It is clear that in the face of something which makes personal problems seem petty, people tend to put them aside. Such good effects do not decide the matter one way or the other.

I do not want to sound churlish or too negative. I rejoice in the good effects. When personal relationships improve in churches, that is good. But it should not and cannot be treated as a test. The 'Toronto Blessing' has had a number of good effects. But they do not prove that the 'Blessing' is a move of the Holy Spirit. We all know that when something happens good effects may result, even if the initial event is not good in itself.

Good people, on the other hand, will show that they are good by their deeds and words (their 'good fruit'), while evil people will produce evil deeds and words. This is what the New Testament tells us we should look out for—not the so-called 'fruit' of a movement, but the fruit in a person's life. The New Testament teaches us to test a person, particularly a person who aspires to leadership, by their words and deeds. It is no accident that the most famous passage in the New Testament on fruit, Gal. 5.22-23, is about these personal qualities. It is about the character of those people who have the Spirit of Christ in them: 'the fruit of the Spirit is love, joy, peace, patience, kindness, goodness, faithfulness, gentleness, self-control'.

What, then, does the New Testament teach us about 'building up the church'?

Building up the Church

This idea is found mainly in 1 Corinthians. As we have seen, Paul in this letter is dealing with the problem that the Corinthian Christians tend to set too much store by outwardly spiritual manifestations. In particular, they assign too much prestige to those who speak in tongues, thinking that such a strange manifestation must be a sign of great inward spirituality. It seems that, as a result, church meetings are being taken over by too much speaking in tongues. Paul does not want exercise of the gift to halt altogether, but he does want it to be controlled; when it is exercised, there should be an interpretation given so that others present can understand and receive from it (see 14.27-28).

Paul seeks to make the Corinthians understand that, when Christians are gathered together, they should focus not on themselves and what they can get from the meeting but on what they can give to each other. They are all part of the one body, and each part works for the good of the whole, not for itself (see 12.12-26). Each of them is to do this with an attitude of self-giving love, the kind of love described in 1 Corinthians 13.

Within this context, Paul urges the Corinthians to operate their spiritual gifts in a manner that will 'build up' others. Speaking in tongues is rather unsuited to this because it only 'builds up' or 'edifies' the person speaking in tongues, unless an interpretation is given, in which case others can benefit. So Paul would rather that speaking in tongues be done in private (14.19) or, if in public, that an interpretation follow (14.28). Much better, he thinks, are the gifts which *de facto* operate for the sake of others, such as prophecy (14.4). These gifts build up the church.

How might this understanding of 'building up' be applied to the 'Toronto Blessing'? I do not think we can apply it directly to the strange physical phenomena since nobody, as far as I am aware, is claiming that these are 'spiritual gifts'. People do not claim to be operating them, rather they claim they are being 'operated on'. However, it would be salutary to remember that, in Paul's view, Christians ought to attend meetings and take part in them, not in order to have themselves 'built up' but in order to build others up. The tendency of people to go to meetings to 'drink in' and 'soak up' blessing, to do what has come to be called 'carpet-time', seems to be a long way from what Paul envisaged for the church. Whatever conclusion we come to about the 'Blessing', this is an important point.

It is also important to realise that 'building up' is supposed to be a way of living, not a way of testing experiences and religious movements. We should seek to edify others in all we say and do.[27] 'Make love your aim', says Paul. This leads us to a key issue: it seems to me that the New Testament wants Christians to concentrate on motives and attitudes, not on tangible results. The New Testament urges us to focus on how we do things, not on what we get of them. It urges us to 'make love our aim', to do good deeds and say good things, and let the results take care of themselves. Advocates of the 'Toronto Blessing', however, base their arguments on results. They have bought into our modern, success-orientated culture. Just like modern technology, the 'Toronto Blessing' seems to achieve results. 'Blessing' supporters talk of greater numbers attending meetings, of people being 'refreshed', of people becoming more excited about Christianity, and so on.

Think, in contrast, of the seven churches in the book of Revelation. It is in terms of their character and deeds that they are either commended or rebuked. It is the means that matter, not the results. The last two of the seven are prime examples in this regard. Of the sixth, the church in Philadelphia, the Lord says,

> *I know your works. Behold, I have set before you an open door, which no one is able to shut; I know that you have but little power, and yet you have kept my word and have not denied my name.* (Rev. 3.8).

It seems that in their own eyes, and presumably in the eyes of the world, this was a rather pathetic little church with little to show for itself. Yet, in the midst of suffering, it had the character to patiently endure in obedience to God (see 3.10). It is commended for this, and the Lord has nothing to say against it. Significantly, the only other church of the seven for which the Lord has no rebuke is the church at Smyrna, a church which only knows tribulation and poverty (see 2.9).

The seventh church, on the other hand, the church in Laodicea, considers itself to be highly successful: 'You say, "I am rich, I have prospered, and I need nothing"' (3.17). It is a church which sees itself as having achieved 'results'. But the Lord sees matters differently: he says to the church, '... you are wretched, pitiable, poor, blind, and naked'. He sees what humans cannot see, that the church is neither hot, nor cold, but lukewarm. The situation is very similar with the church in Sardis, to whom the Lord says, 'you have the name of being alive, and you are dead' (3.1).

Finally, notice some of the other things that the seven churches are commended or rebuked for. The Christians in Ephesus are commended because they 'cannot bear evil men but have tested those who call themselves apostles but are not, and found them to be false' (2.2), while those in Pergamum are rebuked for having some among them 'who hold the teaching of Balaam' and others 'who hold the teaching of the Nicolaitans' (2.14-15). Those in Thyatira are rebuked for tolerating 'the woman Jezebel, who calls herself a prophetess and is teaching and beguiling my servants to practice immorality and to eat food sacrificed to idols' (2.20). Clearly, what sort of leaders churches allow in their midst is crucially important. What matters is not whether they 'get results', but whether they are false or evil—whether they teach false or evil things, which lead others astray. This is what Christians should be testing, not 'results'. Churches should be seeking not to 'be successful', but in times of suffering to patiently endure like the church at Philadelphia, and in times of prosperity and success to ensure that they are not lukewarm, that they are not dead when they appear alive. It is character, words and deeds that are to be our concern: what 'results' we get, individually or corporately, proves nothing.

Conclusion

In this chapter I have dealt with the most important part of the debate over the 'Toronto Blessing'—the argument about 'fruit'. It is an argument which at first sounds as though it must be biblical. But it is made up of various strands which, when they are unravelled, do not measure up to New Testament teaching. We have seen that looking at testimonies about spiritual experiences and their results is not the same as either John's 'testing the spirits' or Paul's 'discerning the spirits'. We have also seen that, in any case, the New Testament concept of 'fruit' is rather different from the idea of 'spiritual results' which is used to justify the 'Blessing'. Therefore, I conclude that those who advocate the 'Toronto Blessing' on the basis of 'the fruit argument' do so without biblical support, despite appearances to the contrary.

NOTES

1. *The Impact of Toronto* (Crowborough: Monarch, 1995), pp. 25-26.
2. *Catch the Fire* (London: Marshall Pickering, 1994), pp. 52-53.
3. *Times of Refreshing* (London: Marshall Pickering, 1995), p. 36.
4. Ibid, pp. 36-39.
5. Ibid, p. 39.
6. Ibid, p. 43.
7. Ibid, p. 44.
8. I presume this is what David Pytches thinks when he speaks of the enormous variety of strange sounds that are evident in some 'Blessing' meetings and says, 'The leadership of the church will be given the wisdom and discernment to deal with these "sounds". Use of the word 'discernment' here is deliberate, because whatever God does the enemy will try to simulate' in 'The Blessings and the Concerns' [*Renewal* magazine; number 223, December 1994], pp. 15-16.
9. Some people argue that the phrase 'but test everything' refers not only to all prophecy, but to every spiritual matter. It is impossible to know for sure which position is correct, but for the sake of my discussion it does not matter, since on both interpretations Paul is urging that prophecy be tested.
10. G. Fee, *The First Epistle to the Corinthians* (NICNT; Grand Rapids, MI: Eerdmans, 1987), p. 596.
11. Idem.
12. Ibid, p. 597.
13. *Times of Refreshing*, p. 37.
14. Idem.
15. G. Fee, *The First Epistle to the Corinthians*, p. 557.
16. Ibid, p. 578 (my italics).
17. Fee puts it this way: 'Paul's point in context is not to establish a means of "testing the spirits," but to remind them that "inspired utterance" as such is not evidence of being led of the Spirit.' Ibid, p. 581.
18. *Times of Refreshing*, p. 44.
19. Ibid, p. 38.
20. *Catch the Fire*, p. 53.
21. *Times of Refreshing*, p. 38.
22. Idem.
23. Ibid, p. 43.

24. Ibid, p. 39.
25. Idem.
26. Idem.
27. This does not bar us, by the way, from saying hard, critical things to one another when necessary. Paul does precisely this regularly in his letters. But hard, critical things should be said with the aim of 'building up'.

CHAPTER 5

God-Given Reason

A very noticeable feature of the 'Toronto Blessing' has been the tendency among those involved to play down the role of reason. One aspect of this attitude has taken the form of solemn warnings against analysis. Analysis, it is said, will prevent us from receiving. When we analyse we place a barrier between ourselves and what God wants to do in us.

I will return to the role of analysis later. However, there is more to the issue than meets the eye. A view has developed that some Christians are not receiving the 'Blessing' because they are too influenced by the modern Western preference for rationality above experience, and by the accompanying disbelief of the miraculous. It is thought that these Christians have been culturally conditioned by the eighteenth-century Enlightenment ideal of autonomous reason: they think too much. The upshot of this view is that any reasoning—any argument—offered in criticism of the 'Toronto Blessing' becomes suspect. 'We have experienced the Holy Spirit,' goes the cry, 'don't try to argue with our experience.' Such pleas must be resisted. As I intend to show, they are at root unchristian: reasoning and argument are, in fact, New Testament ideals, and as such precede the Enlightenment by seventeen centuries. I will show that the need to analyse the 'Toronto Blessing' is a Christian one, not a modern culturally conditioned one.

Reason in the New Testament

Why do I say that the use of our reason is a New Testament ideal? Many of Paul's letters contain portions of sustained argument. Paul reasons with the Christians in Galatia as to why they should not go along with the new teaching of the 'judaisers' who have come among them, and should instead remain true to the gospel he preached to them. He argues with the Corinthian Christians about the need to place unity and love above shows of charismatic power. His letter to the Romans is one of the greatest pieces of extended argument in the whole of the world's literature. In fact, not only Paul's letters, but all the New Testament epistles, contain instances of reasons given as to why Christians should do and believe some things and not others.

Jesus, of course, taught 'as one who had authority, and not as the scribes' (Mk 1.22). As the Son of God, he did not have to justify what he said (although anyone reading through his teachings will see that he usually did provide explanations—often in the form of parables—and not just pronouncements). However, neither Paul nor the other apostles considered themselves to have the kind of authority Jesus had. It was not their prerogative to simply state whether a thing was good or bad, right or wrong. Instead, they gave reasons to their fellow Christians as to why they had reached certain conclusions and decisions (see, for example, Acts 15.1-21).

Surely, then, we too are called upon to understand why we believe and to consider the justification for claims others make. Thus Peter tells his readers to be ready to give a defence 'for the hope that is in you' (1 Pet. 3.15), while the Berean Jews are commended for subjecting Paul's preaching to careful scrutiny (Acts 17.11).

Experience and Reason

I said a moment ago that Christians who dislike the strange phenomena of the 'Toronto Blessing' are often accused of being culturally conditioned by the Enlightenment—placing reason above experience. What they should do, it is argued, is embrace the experiences which God has given and then use their reason to understand them. According to this argument, Enlightenment-influenced Christians have reversed the correct relationship: they need to realise that experience comes first, reason second. This is often put in terms of 'receiving' versus 'theologizing'. On numerous occasions, people promoting the 'Toronto Blessing' have said such things as, 'If your theology is stopping you receiving, then you need to change your theology. Once you have received, then your theology needs to change in order to accommodate the strangeness of your new experience.' This sort of view is common. But what does the New Testament say?

The first thing to note is that 'experience' is not a New Testament word. Until the nineteenth century, 'experience' meant what we now mean by the word 'experiment'.[1] The modern understanding of experience seems to have arisen in reaction to the equally modern notion of rationality. In this understanding, human reason is seen as being isolated from the rest of human life. Humans are supposedly able to think rationally, without their thoughts being influenced by what they are, what they have done, where they live, and so on. The Enlightenment Mind, in other words, can be completely objective, unbiased, uninfluenced by outside forces. It is cool and detached.[2] Once this understanding had arisen, a 'place' had to be found for human sensations and emotions, as well as for such things as love and hate. These came to be regarded as

105

located in the realm of 'experience', a realm separate from rationality. Once that had happened the classic modern divide between reason and experience, 'heart' and 'head', was here to stay.

Ironically, therefore, those who argue that experience should be placed above reason are themselves radically influenced by the Enlightenment mind-set, even when they criticise others for giving reason too high a place. They have accepted Enlightenment categories and merely reversed them. In so doing, they have followed a well-trodden path, a path that was laid down by the Romanticist movement in the eighteenth century. The Romantics reacted against the intellectualism and formal restraint engendered by the Enlightenment during the previous century. They used the arts to emphasise the importance of imagination and emotions, and gave them a higher place than reason and formality.

The New Testament View

The New Testament view is very different from the view embraced by the Enlightenment and its Romanticist reaction. In the New Testament, the mind is not detached from the rest of what we are. Rather, it is an integral part of our personality. That is why Paul says, 'be transformed by the renewal of your mind' (Rom. 12.2). As our minds are renewed, the whole of our being is transformed. This does not mean that somehow the Holy Spirit supernaturally works on our brain cells to give us better brains. Rather, it means that we should strive to understand the truth about what God has done for us in Jesus Christ, and so move from a non-Christian understanding of God and the world to a Christian one. Thus, Paul precedes Romans 12 with eleven chapters of explanation of what he believes God has done in Christ, eleven chapters of theology. He structures Romans in this way because he is convinced that, as the people to whom he writes begin to 'believe rightly', their minds will be renewed and thus their whole beings will be transformed. Indeed, all Paul's letters contain large portions of (at times very difficult) theology, particularly when things are going wrong in the church to which he is writing. This reflects his conviction that what we *are* is intimately connected to what we *think*.

John's Gospel is written for similar reasons: 'Now Jesus did many other signs in the presence of the disciples, which are not written in this book; but these are written that you may believe that Jesus is the Christ, the Son of God, and that believing you may have life in his name' (Jn. 20.30-31). Believing the truth—in this case the most important truth of all, that Jesus is the Christ, the Son of God—enables us to live the life God intends for us.

What we believe determines what we do and how we behave. We must resist the Enlightenment view of the mind: mind cannot be detached from experience. It is a mistake for Christians to think that what they believe does not really matter so long as they are getting the 'right experiences'. Yet that is precisely what many involved in the 'Blessing' do think. A case in point is the attitude towards Rodney Howard-Browne, an itinerant charismatic minister. Howard-Browne is not directly connected with the Toronto Vineyard church at which the 'Blessing' began. (The Vineyard leaders did, however, go to his meetings in the months before the 'Blessing' came to Toronto, in order to 'tap in' to the power his ministry manifested.[3]) Nevertheless, his ministry displays the same kind of phenomena as are seen in the 'Blessing'. So, although he holds to a number of unorthodox doctrines and is connected with the (perhaps heretical[4]) Faith Movement, his ministry is affirmed by proponents of the 'Blessing'. Here is what Gerald Coates has to say about a video he watched of a Howard-Browne meeting:

> Howard-Browne began to 'work' the audience, and literally dozens of people laughed and fell. Only a handful failed to fall when Howard-Browne touched them, one or two looked possibly to have been pushed, and some seemed to fall down because it was 'expected' of them. Yet the majority of people seemed to have been genuinely 'slain in the Spirit' in a spontaneous manner—in spite of Copeland's suspect theology, and Howard-Browne's unwise association with the Faith Movement's heir apparent. I had no doubt that I was watching genuine spiritual activity at work, despite the 'punch line' where Copeland touched Howard-Browne, and the stocky evangelist himself hit the deck![5]

Journalist Mike Fearon recites an account concerning one of the founding leaders of the 'Blessing', Randy Clark:

> [When he] set out to receive the ministry of Rodney Howard-Browne, he was at first troubled to learn that Howard-Browne's next meetings were to take place in Kenneth Hagin Jr's Rhema Bible church in Tulsa: A church with whose teachings Clark had doctrinal disagreements [sc. because Hagin is heavily involved in the Faith Movement, a movement which, as Fearon puts it, is 'heretical and cultish']. Clark believed that God disapproved of his own smug, denominational attitudes. He went along and received ministry, in spite of his own theological reservations.[6]

I have not quoted these examples in order to raise the issue of Howard-Browne's involvement in the 'Blessing' (though it is important, as I will show later). My purpose is to show that an attitude has developed in which right belief—theology, doctrine, call it what we will—is treated as being almost irrelevant, so long as the experience is right.

Consider how Coates and Clark felt able to judge what they witnessed in these two cases as being 'good'. In the first example, Coates was watching a video of a meeting which had taken place some time before. He could therefore only go by what he saw on the screen. According to what he says, the way Howard-Browne and Copeland acted and what they said did not tell him that this was good. In fact all of the 'theological indicators' pointed in the opposite direction. The only thing which can have told him that what was going on was 'good' was that people fell and laughed 'spontaneously'. Presumably, Coates means by this that their laughter and falling were due neither to their own prior decision nor to some other human cause, such as being pushed. So, on the basis of having seen people fall and laugh 'spontaneously', Coates judges that 'genuine spiritual activity' was 'at work'. How can this be? How, once theological indicators have been discounted, can the sight of strange but nevertheless purely physical phenomena tell us anything about spiritual activity?

The second case is similar, only, this time, Randy Clark did not judge by watching a video. Presumably, he heard reports that strange and powerful things were happening in Howard-Browne's meetings. He wanted to experience this power, so he went to a meeting despite his profound theological disagreements with the host-church's leader, Hagin. Again, his judgement was based on what he saw happen, not on his theological perceptions.

Finally in considering these two examples, notice a crucial feature. Fearon says, 'Clark believed that God disapproved of his own smug, denominational attitudes.' This can only mean that, in Clark's view, God himself thought that

Clark's theological reservations were irrelevant in the face of what could be experienced at the meetings. Similarly for Coates, 'genuine spiritual activity' takes place despite the theological problems. This is representative of the prevailing belief that God is at work in the experiential realm, and that the rational, intellectual realm is virtually irrelevant.

I am not suggesting we ought to believe the opposite, namely that the intellectual realm is what counts, that we must not expect to 'experience' God. As a charismatic Christian, I strongly believe that God is active in every part of our life, and that many of the spiritual gifts have an outward, physical side. It is important that his influence is not confined to cerebral matters. My criticism is that the division into two distinct spheres is wrong in the first place. The human being is one undivided whole. Belief and experience, thought and action are intimately connected. It is sometimes useful to talk about things as though there were 'two realms', but it can also be very misleading. Moreover it is dangerous to argue that spirituality can be divorced from belief. We are saved by faith *in Christ*, not by faith in Mohammed, or even by faith in whatever it is that makes people fall over and laugh uncontrollably. To be sure, faith in Christ is more than mere intellectual assent to the Creeds. It is living, active trust in the one who came and died for us. But intellectual belief is a vital part of it: in order for me to trust in Christ, I must have an intellectual conception of who he is. That is why our evangelism does not consist purely of the words, 'Believe in Jesus.' We tell people *about* Jesus, who he was, what he did. Only then are they able to believe in him.

The need for intellectual belief does not stop there. It is necessary to the whole of our Christian life. Our growth as Christians, our sanctification, is especially dependent on what we believe. That is why Paul said, 'be transformed *by the renewal of your mind*'. It is also why, in the Gospel of John, Jesus asks the Father to, 'Sanctify them in the truth; thy word is truth' (17.17). 'Truth' is a crucial concept in John's Gospel:

> *'If you continue in my word, you are truly my disciples, and you will know the truth, and the truth will make you free'*
>
> (8.31-32).

This is not 'any old truth'—knowledge of scientific truth, for example, will not set us free—it is truth which is available to us only in our faith relationship with Jesus:

> *'I am the way, and the truth, and the life; no one comes to the Father, but by me'* (14.6).

It is truth which the Holy Spirit brings to us:

> *'And I will pray the Father, and he will give you another Counsellor, to be with you for ever, even the Spirit of truth, whom the world cannot receive, because it neither sees him nor knows him; you know him, for he dwells with you, and will be in you'* (14.16-17).

> *'When the Spirit of truth comes, he will guide you into all the truth'* (16.13).

It is what we might call 'relational truth', which comes to us by the Holy Spirit. But it is still *truth*, and so it can only be apprehended by our God-given reason. It is something our minds come to know, not something we feel. This is the mistake many people who are involved in the 'Toronto Blessing' have made. They have thought that God can be 'experienced' in a way which makes reason irrelevant. Some people have even been advised not to allow their concern for the truth to prevent them from receiving the 'Blessing'.

Conclusion

This book is written in the conviction that where God is, truth is. I do not consider myself to have a complete grasp of the truth. None of us has that. But we do all have the Bible, and the Bible is testimony to truth. It is testimony to Jesus Christ, the Word of God. It tells us about the things God has done for us in Jesus Christ; and that is the truth.

NOTES
1. Leslie Newbiggin has some important things to say on this matter in his 'Truth and Authority in Modernity', in P. Sampson, V. Samuel and C. Sugden (eds.), *Faith and Modernity* (Oxford: Regnum Books, 1994), pp. 60-88.
2. This understanding is epitomised by René Descartes' famous quest for philosophical certainty, a quest that stands at the heart of modernity. For Descartes, whatever could be doubted could not be certain. And he found that he could doubt almost everything. He could doubt his senses, since he might be dreaming, and the seat on which he felt himself to be sitting might be part of the dream. There was only one thing he could not doubt, and that was the fact of his doubting. It was impossible to doubt that he was doubting. From this simple piece of logic he concluded that he must exist. Because he was doubting (or, more generally, thinking), he knew that he existed. So came his famous formula, *cogito ergo sum*: 'I think, therefore I am.' With this idea, 'thinking' is seen as being isolated from everything else. And so 'pure thought' came to dominate the modern concept of rationality.
3. See G. Chevreau, *Catch the Fire* (London: Marshall Pickering, 1994), p. 23.
4. See T. Smail, A. Walker and N. Wright, '"Revelation Knowledge" and Knowledge of Revelation: The Faith Movement and the Question of Heresy', *Journal of Pentecostal Theology* 5 (October 1994), pp. 57-77.
5. In M. Fearon, *A Breath of Fresh Air* (Guildford: Eagle, 1994), pp. 122-23.
6. Ibid, pp. 105-106.

CHAPTER 6

Testing the Spirits

In the remaining chapters I will attempt to set out a biblical evaluation of the 'Toronto Blessing'. In offering such an evaluation it is difficult to know where to begin. There are so many aspects to, and features of, the 'Blessing' which need to be considered, and so many ways of looking at them, that no single approach is likely to be adequate. It would be extremely useful, for example, to be able to offer sociological and historical analyses. But my area of study is theology and Bible interpretation, so it is from that angle that I will approach the subject.

The obvious place to start is with the biblical tests I described in Chapter 4. I argued there that proponents of the 'Blessing' have misunderstood and misapplied these tests. How then should they be applied?

Biblical Testing

Perhaps the key finding of my analysis in Chapter 4 was that the biblical tests are not intended to be applied to the results or effects (what has come to be known as the 'fruit') of Christian movements and ministries, telling us whether these movements and ministries are 'of God'. Rather, they are intended to be applied to individual people. Let us look at how they work.

1 John 4

> *Beloved, do not believe every spirit, but test the spirits to see whether they are of God (v. 1).*

I showed in Chapter 4 that this very important text reminds us of the need to be sure that people who display manifestations of power are only allowed influence in Christian communities if they hold to right beliefs and live accordingly. This is what I would call a 'test of orthodoxy'. Only those people whose confession is orthodox, and whose lives are in line with their confession, should be allowed positions of influence in Christian churches.

Despite what a number of 'Blessing' supporters have said, it is entirely wrong to think that a person's orthodoxy does not really matter as long as they are doing 'spiritually powerful things'. In such instances especially, their orthodoxy is crucial, since the spiritual power they manifest will be very damaging if it is not operated under the Lordship of Christ. By 'orthodoxy' I do not mean 'correctness in every tiny aspect of belief'. Nor do I mean 'those beliefs which agree with mine'. What I mean is something like the 'mere Christianity' which C.S. Lewis talked about. As Andrew Walker puts it, Lewis

> insisted that there is a common path of Christianity that pilgrims down the ages have trod in the certainty that they were on firm ground. This ground was for Lewis the high road of basic orthodoxy, the great viaduct of Christendom that proudly and surely has spanned the changes and uncertainties of the centuries. Christians—mere Christians—can recognise each other on the way, and while they may argue and fail to agree on many matters, they are nevertheless travellers together on 'the main road'.[1]

One of the features of this 'main road' is what Walker calls 'a broad Trinitarian orthodoxy'.[2] So, if somebody who was influential in the origins of the 'Toronto Blessing' were found to be teaching something substantially contrary to Trinitarian orthodoxy, there would be a case for saying that they should not have been allowed such influence. There is reason to suspect this is exactly what has happened. I am thinking of the teachings of Benny Hinn. For a time, Hinn taught that there are nine members of the Trinity. He subsequently recanted the teaching, but this does not alter the fact that *while he was teaching it* he was allowed a considerable degree of influence in Christian circles in North America, including Toronto. Guy Chevreau tells us,

> In September of 1992, Carol and John [Arnott, the main pastors of Toronto Airport Vineyard] went to several meetings of Benny Hinn's in Toronto. John had become friends with Benny years ago, at the outset of his ministry in Toronto. Longing for a similar kind of empowerment ... they joined the crowd at Maple Leaf Gardens.[3]

We can presume that this account is accurate, since John Arnott provides the Preface to Chevreau's book, in which he thoroughly endorses what Chevreau says. In my opinion, the Arnotts failed to 'test the spirits' properly in this case. Despite the manifestations of power they saw at Hinn's meetings, they should not have given his ministry influence in their lives and sought for his kind of 'empowerment'. This is not a denunciation of Hinn, or even a definitive statement about him as a Christian leader. I merely raise his case as an example of where, judging from their own accounts of the matter, the 'founders' of the 'Toronto Blessing' failed to 'test the spirits' properly.

As we saw in Chapter 5, Randy Clark, another of the 'founders' of the 'Blessing', almost applied the test, but in the end failed to do so.

> [Clark] was at first troubled to learn that Howard-Browne's next meetings were to take place in Kenneth Hagin Jr's Rhema Bible church in Tulsa: A church with whose teachings Clark had doctrinal disagreements.[4]

Unfortunately, he eventually 'went along and received ministry, in spite of his own theological reservations'. He 'believed that God disapproved of his own smug, denominational attitudes'.[5] Of course, if Clark did have a 'bad attitude' then he needed to change it. To use a cliché, however, two wrongs do not make a right. The 'cure' for his bad attitude was surely not for him to go and receive ministry from somebody whose confession was suspect.

I say 'confession' because with Howard-Browne it is not merely a case of suspect theology: there are also questions of suspect practice. In the video tapes I have seen of Howard-Browne's meetings, there is very little explicitly-stated theology to make judgements about. However, in my view, what he *does* in his meetings is extremely questionable. It would not be appropriate to go into this in more detail here since this book is about the 'Toronto Blessing', not Rodney Howard-Browne. My point is that, if the manner in which he conducts his meetings is not in line with Christian belief, then he should not be allowed influence in Christian communities. Where Howard-Browne is concerned this is all the more important, since he has undoubtedly been one of the major sources of the 'Blessing'. As Dave Roberts puts it, 'a key piece at the centre of the picture is Rodney Howard-Browne'.[6] Indeed, while the Toronto Airport Vineyard has been an extremely important catalyst in the coming of 'Blessing' phenomena to Britain, these phenomena were already occurring elsewhere in the world independently of events in Toronto. A consensus has developed that the wave of strange physical phenomena which characterises the 'Blessing' does not have its source in Toronto, but rather in the ministry of Howard-Browne.

The sequence of events seems to have been as follows: in early 1993, Randy Clark attended Howard-Browne meetings, and lined up:

> repeatedly to receive prayer. Five months later, [Howard-Browne] discerned a powerful anointing being released in Randy's life—he came over to him and said, "This is the fire of God in your hands; go home and pray for everyone in your church." The first Sunday of Randy's return, he did as instructed, and saw a similar outbreak of the Spirit as he ministered.[7]

Soon after, Clark was invited to visit Toronto Airport Vineyard and minister there.

In June 1993, John and Carol Arnott attended a Howard-Browne meeting in Texas. John Arnott stood in a line for 'prayer' from Howard-Browne but, while all others in the line fell 'under the power', Arnott was left standing. In November 1993 John Arnott was prayed for by Claudio Freidzon (who had himself been affected at a Benny Hinn meeting). This time Arnott did fall down.[8]

With respect to what has happened in Britain, it seems that much of the 'Blessing' has come through contacts with Toronto (and so only indirectly through Howard-Browne). However, it has been pointed out that a number of churches received phenomena through direct contacts with Howard-Browne.

In April 1994, Charles and Francis Hunter ministered at Kensington Temple, London, and 'Blessing'-type phenomena broke out. According to Kensington Temple's leader, Colin Dye, the Hunters 'had been with Rodney

Howard-Browne; in fact most of what has happened can be traced to what the Lord began to do through Rodney.'[9]

Also in April 1994, members of Terry Virgo's church in Columbia, USA, attended Howard-Browne meetings. They took the manifestations back to the church.[10] Then, in the spring and early summer of 1994, Howard-Browne prayed for Terry Virgo and another influential British church, leader Bryn Jones.[11]

In May 1994, Virgo and his co-leader Dave Holden (who had also been prayed for by Howard-Browne in April) returned to Britain to join a New Frontiers International leaders' retreat. The phenomena broke out there, and subsequently in the home churches of the 250 leaders who had been present.[12]

I think it is fair to say that, if the Toronto leadership had properly 'tested the spirits' with respect to Howard-Browne, he would probably have been found wanting. If proper testing had been carried out, he would not have been allowed the influence he has had. Consequently, there might not then have been a *Toronto* 'Blessing'. If British church leaders had done the same, the phenomena would not have had anything like the impact they have had here.

Matthew 7.15-16

Beware of false prophets, who come to you in sheep's clothing but inwardly are ravenous wolves. You will know them by their fruits.

As we saw in Chapter 4, Jesus is here warning that people with deceptively powerful ministries would emerge in the first churches. The situation is no different today. Such people then must be watched for, and assessed on the basis of their character as it is revealed by their behaviour, words and deeds.

Ideally, of course, assessment would take place within the local church. People who are looking for influence within these communities would find their private lives under scrutiny. Their actions and words would be liable to assessment. Their fellow Christians would seek to discover whether they were seeking to serve the church or their own interests. Unfortunately, today this kind of assessment is often difficult. We are frequently able to see only the public face of the most 'charismatic' figures. In these circumstances it is my view that the test of character ought to be applied rigorously. If there appear to be reasons to doubt their character we should deny such figures any influence over us.

The case of Rodney Howard-Browne is illustrative of what I mean. He has an itinerant ministry in the United States, with apparently no local church base. The vast majority of Christians in Britain will have been able to assess him only on the basis of his 'public face'. This 'public face' consists of books he has written and videos of his meetings. In both of these media, there are apparent reasons to doubt Howard-Browne. Yet, in the last two or three years he has been warmly welcomed on to the British church scene.

What do I mean by 'apparent reasons to doubt'? There are his strong personal connections with the Faith Movement, and his embracing of some of the Faith Movement's false teachings. Dave Roberts (in an article which appears to be in favour of Howard-Browne) tells us, 'Those willing to comb Rodney's books will find Word of Faith style comments.'[13] This is a sign that Howard-Browne may be unorthodox, and so may fail the 1 John 4 test. In my opinion, videos of Howard-Browne's meetings reveal signs that he may also fail the test of character. In his videos, Howard-Browne appears to manipulate and humiliate people for the sake of impressing

119

the audience with his 'spiritual powers'. He also seems prepared to use spiritual gifts to the same end. In one video he engages in an extended, private (that is, uninterpreted) 'conversation' in tongues with the meeting's host, Kenneth Copeland. At one point in the 'conversation', they even appear to be telling each other jokes in tongues.[14]

These reasons to doubt do not in themselves prove that Howard-Browne would fail the tests of character and of orthodoxy. I do not know enough about him to make a judgement on that. But I do believe that, because of the evidence on open display, he should not have been given the benefit of the doubt and welcomed on to the platforms of British churches. Instead he should have been held at arm's length. Because he has a 'powerful ministry', British leaders such as Gerald Coates have commended Howard-Browne. Having watched the video discussed above, Coates comments,

> the congregation was treated to the duo "hamming it up" like a pair of slapstick comics in burlesque. Their "tongues" sounded totally un-convincing, and the American style was an embarrassing echo of all that is worse in banal tele-evangelism.

But even so,

> I had no doubt that I was watching genuine spiritual activity at work, despite the "punchline" where Copeland touched Howard-Browne, and the stocky evangelist himself hit the deck![15]

For Coates, what seems to matter is that Howard-Browne 'gets results'—people fall over, laugh and so on. As I have already made clear, what ought to matter are the signs of dubious character and questionable orthodoxy. These are what the New Testament counsels us to look out for. I explained in Chapter 4 why 'getting results' ought not to sway us. This is worth re-emphasising with some words drawn, ironically, from Coates himself:

> Manifestations, of course, provide no indication of the spiritual value of the work.[16]

It is difficult to conceive how somebody who knows this could state that what he saw on the Howard-Browne video was 'genuine spiritual activity'. It may well have been powerful activity, but the signs are that it was not *genuine spiritual* activity.

Behaving Charitably

On reading what I have said in this Chapter, many people will think that I am being uncharitable. Is what I have said really in the spirit of Christian love and tolerance? I believe it is. Christians are called to love one another and tolerate what they consider to be faults in others—we are called to be charitable. But in my view, this is the attitude we are called to have towards others *as fellow Christians*. When people seek to gain influence over us, however other factors also come into play. Such people must expect to be treated with considerable rigour. And when they do not come from a local church context and we have no knowledge of them except their 'public face', they must expect yet more rigorous examination.

Of course, if somebody like Rodney Howard-Browne came to a local church seeking only fellowship and the opportunity to worship with others, then he ought to be shown proper Christian tolerance. Signs that he may hold unorthodox beliefs and have some character faults ought to be treated with patience and love. But Howard-Browne has not come to British churches on that basis. Rather, he has come seeking to have influence over people who have never met him and who know him only through his publicity. He has brought a ministry which (whether we think it is good or bad) can be accurately described as highly 'invasive' in terms of individuals' spirituality.

It may be that in relation to such people we will err on the side of caution. However, that is the way it ought to be. If they are Christians they will know that they do not have an automatic right to take their ministry wherever they wish. And, as Christians, we should be confident that, with God 'on our side' we will not suffer undue harm by failing to receive their ministry. Unfortunately, many Christians do not have that confidence, and 'fear of missing out' seems to cause them to err on the side of laxity.

The point I wish to make is that, while as Christians we must behave charitably towards each other (and towards non-Christians), we must at the same time be rigorous towards those who seek influence and authority. The fact that a person appears to minister in great power ought not to make the slightest difference. Again it is worth noting that the church at Ephesus was commended by the Lord because it refused to 'bear evil men but ... tested those who call themselves apostles but are not, and found them to be false' (Rev. 2.2).

Conclusion

In Chapter 4, I argued that proponents of the 'Toronto Blessing' have misunderstood how the biblical tests of 1 John 4 and Matthew 7 are to be applied. They believe that the tests can be applied to testimonies of those who have been 'blessed' in order to see whether what they have experienced is 'of God'. I showed that the biblical tests are not intended to tell us about the value of what people have experienced, but rather about whether they are Christians and whether they can be trusted as leaders. This tells us how the tests should be applied within ordinary churches that are experiencing the 'Blessing'.

The likelihood is that in many churches people will have risen to prominence because they have received 'amazing things' and because they testify eloquently to what they have 'received'. It is not impossible that such people are not Christians and/or that they are of bad character. Certainly, people who are not Christians have been to meetings at the Toronto Airport Fellowship and have experienced the phenomena. There is the well known case of the Daily Telegraph reporter, Mick Brown, who went there to investigate what was happening. Brown reports how, towards the end of one meeting that he was observing, he found himself

> beside John Arnott ... I didn't even see his hand coming as it arced through the air and touched me gently—hardly at all—on the forehead...I could feel a palpable shock running through me, then I was falling backwards, as if my legs had been kicked away from underneath me.
> I hit the floor—I swear this is the truth—laughing like a drain.[17]

Despite his experience, Brown did not become a Christian. Indeed, in a subsequent interview that he gave to *Evangelicals Now* newspaper, Brown stated that his visit to Toronto made no difference to his view of God, Jesus Christ or Christianity.[18]

Brown did not seek to join a church or have influence within the Christian community, but there is every possibility that there will be people who display 'Blessing'-type

123

phenomena within churches who are not Christians. There is also a real possibility that some people of bad character will seek to make capital of their displays of phenomena to gain position within churches.

Leaving aside the question of what overall judgements we should make about the 'Toronto Blessing', it is in these kinds of circumstance that the tests of 1 John 4 and Matthew 7 need to be applied. In this time of enormous ferment, churches will be wise to apply them diligently.

In terms of the 'Toronto Blessing' itself, I feel it is right to conclude— given what I said earlier in the Chapter—that there is considerable doubt about what we might call its 'source'. Had church leaders in Toronto and Britain applied the biblical tests properly, they would have recognised the dangers and the 'Toronto Blessing' would not have got off the ground. However, that is something of an 'academic point', since the 'Blessing' has come and it has had an enormous impact. The key question now is how we should judge that which is with us.

NOTES

1. A. Walker, 'Introduction', in A. Walker (ed.), *Different Gospels* (London: Hodder & Stoughton, 1988), p. 7.
2. Ibid, p. xii.
3. *Catch the Fire* (London: Marshall Pickering, 1994), p. 22.
4. In Fearon, *A Breath of Fresh Air* (Guildford: Eagle, 1994), pp. 105-106.
5. Ibid, p. 106.
6. D. Roberts, 'The Joyful Power Evangelist', in *Alpha* magazine (December, 1994), p. 5.
7. *Catch the Fire*, pp. 24-25.
8. Ibid, p. 23.
9. *A Breath of Fresh Air*, p. 139.
10. Ibid, p. 125.
11. 'The Joyful Power Evangelist', p. 6.
12. *A Breath of Fresh Air*, p. 125.
13. 'The Joyful Power Evangelist', p. 7.
14. The video is an officially released one of a rally held on 8 May 1993.
15. *A Breath of Fresh Air*, pp. 122-23.
16. Ibid, p. 124.
17. M. Brown, 'Unzipper heaven, Lord. Ha-ha, ho-ho, he-he ...', in *Telegraph Magazine* (Daily Telegraph, London, Saturday December 3, 1994), p. 30.
18. See 'What Happened Next?', in *Evangelicals Now* newspaper (February 1995), pp. 1, 8.

CHAPTER 7

Is it Spiritual?

The 'Toronto Blessing' is something about which great claims have been made. A few call it a Revival but most agree that it cannot be described as such, essentially because people are not becoming Christians in large numbers. Because it is confined to churches, most of those in favour of it call it a Renewal. Nevertheless, many declare that it will soon become a Revival of very great proportions.

The word 'Renewal' is used to indicate the idea that God is doing a work within an explicitly Christian context, a work which causes Christians and churches to begin living as they should—with true commitment and passion. It is usually characterised as a work which causes Christians to increase in faith, to love one another more and to deepen their concern for the lost. Renewal can happen in the lives of a few individuals, or on a small scale within individual churches. It can also happen on a much larger scale, affecting great numbers. When it happens on a larger scale, the expectation arises that it will become Revival, transforming the world outside the church.

The kinds of things which are thought to occur in Renewal are the kinds of things which those involved in the 'Blessing' say are happening. Perhaps the most characteristic idea is that Christians who had previously been spiritually worn out, or tired, 'dry', even 'desperate', have been re-invigorated in their faith. The fact that 'the Blessing' has come to be known as a 'time of refreshing' indicates the centrality of this idea. This is the best place to turn to next.

Spiritual Refreshment?

Toronto Airport Fellowship is a church which believes in and operates spiritual gifts. It is what is usually described as a charismatic church. People who have travelled to Toronto from Britain in order to 'receive' have mostly been charismatic Christians, and the 'Blessing' has come with greatest impact to those churches in Britain that would call themselves Charismatic. Presumably, therefore, Charismatic Renewal and charismatic life had not proved spiritually satisfactory for many people. The 'Blessing' has provided large numbers of these people with something they felt was lacking. That is assumed to be a good thing.

Yet there is a very real problem which needs to be addressed: while the 'Toronto Blessing' is a phenomenon to which people are turning for their perceived spiritual needs, it occurs within churches which profess a selfless faith. Christians are intended to be people who serve God first and then others, yet—to put the matter bluntly—the 'Blessing' tends towards a self-serving direction.

This tension is revealed very clearly in Mark Stibbe's book, *Times of Refreshing*. In a chapter entitled 'Cultural Factors', Stibbe sets out to explain why it might be that God needs to use the extraordinarily strange physical phenomena observed in the 'Blessing'. He argues,

> First-World, Western cultures have evolved into what one might call 'ecstatic or addictive societies'. By that I mean that the contemporary values, fashions, habits, and characteristics of societies like Great Britain promote a lifestyle of ecstatic, mood-altering

and escapist activities. These mood-altering activities are basically anaesthetics which blot out the
realities of life, and which—however briefly—induce
an altered state of consciousness in which our
problems disappear. They are 'tranquillizers' which
remove pain and which help us—for a little while—to
feel good.[1]

Stibbe proceeds to describe the kinds of things which
become addictive for different people: drugs, food, drink,
gambling, shopping, success, sex, vegetarianism, environ-
mentalism and other '-isms', computers, TV, movies, and so
on.

The 'Toronto Blessing' phenomena are, in Stibbe's
view, 'the divine alternative':

Since ours is a largely Dionysian culture—a culture
of addicts looking for ecstasy—God has chosen to
operate during this time of refreshing by permitting
many ecstatic phenomena—such as shaking,
fainting, falling over, weeping, laughing, roaring, and
generally drunken behaviour.[2]

Leaving aside the question of whether they really are
God's alternative, I agree with Stibbe that the phenomena are
providing what is perceived to be a legitimate religious
alternative. As such, the 'Blessing' has become something to
which many people feel they can return again and again.
Toronto Airport Fellowship has been running its meetings six
nights a week for many months because there is great demand
for what the 'Blessing' has to offer. The demand arises not
only from first-time visitors, but also from those who return
repeatedly. A significant number of the testimonies recorded
in Guy Chevreau's book, *Catch the Fire*, confirm how people
who have been 'Blessed' in Toronto have made repeated
visits over extended periods, to 'receive' more and more.

The same thing has happened in British churches that have become centres for the 'Blessing'.

If the ecstatic experiences which people are undergoing are indeed given by God, and are legitimate spiritual alternatives to what society offers, then there seems no logical reason why people should not do this. If God is pouring out his blessings, then for many people the correct thing to do is to continue receiving what he offers. Yet many of the proponents are uncomfortable with people just 'drinking in' more and more. They know that genuine Christian faith is orientated to giving, not taking.

This is the root of the tension I referred to earlier. In Stibbe's book, it is resolved by the extraordinary claim that, in addition to critics being in danger of the unforgivable sin, those who love the 'Blessing' too much are also in danger. On the basis of Lk. 12.10, Stibbe says that blasphemy against the Holy Spirit can come not just from those who criticise, but also from those who keep going back for more and do not begin to give out despite their new lease of spiritual life.[3]

Stibbe rightly wants Christians who have enjoyed the 'Blessing' to focus their energies on witnessing. However, it seems to me, this desire has led him into an extremely dubious piece of Bible interpretation. I do not intend to go into the details of his interpretation, since it ought to be obvious to everybody who looks at it that it is speculative in the extreme. The key point for us is that it reveals what a serious problem this tension between 'taking' and 'giving' represents. Stibbe says,

> there are those who have been blessed by the Toronto phenomenon and who have received a new lease of spiritual life—those, in other words, who have been to meetings and experienced God's Spirit in a

new way. Some members of this group are in particular danger of misunderstanding the whole purpose of the blessing. I have heard it said by a number of leaders that we are to get as much of the blessing as possible, that we are to keep on going to meetings to be filled, and that we are to receive as much as we can while it is here.[4]

The fact of the matter is that 'the whole purpose of the blessing' is not at all obvious. To many people, 'Blessing' experiences are addictive, and God is not telling them that that is wrong. They go back for more and they get more! Since they believe that God is giving them the experiences, it is logical for them to assume that he wants them to have them. Put simply, if God wanted them to stop going back for more, then he would stop giving the experiences. This is what I call 'the logic of the experience'.

What we have is a conflict between 'the logic of the experience' and 'the logic of Christian theology'. The 'logic of Christian theology' is: 'the reason why we are filled with the Holy Spirit is so that we can give inspired witness to the rich truths of the Good News. The power of the Spirit is not given for self-gratification but for mission (Acts 1:8).'[5]

This reveals something extremely significant. Namely that the claim cannot be maintained that the God of Christian theology is the direct cause of the strange physical phenomena we are seeing. The plain fact is that people can engage in these phenomena as often as they like and for as long as they like. No matter whether leaders such as Mark Stibbe say they should not: the experience remains available to them.

Indeed, it is difficult to see where Stibbe and others like him wish the lines to be drawn. They thoroughly endorse Christians engaging in 'Blessing' experiences, they consider the experiences to be entirely legitimate spiritual activities, yet they do not want Christians to engage in them too much. One way to unravel this conundrum would be to take Stibbe's parallel between addictive experiences offered by society and 'Blessing' experiences a little further. It is perfectly in order for Christians to engage to an extent in society's experiences, but not so far as to become 'addicted'. It is in order for Christians to watch TV or listen to music, for example, so long as the activity does not become all-consuming. Watching TV is a legitimate activity for Christians to engage in, but it must not impinge upon their commitment to the Christian life of witness to, and service of, others.

It could similarly be argued by supporters of the 'Blessing' that Christians can engage legitimately in 'Blessing' phenomena, so long as the engagement does not detract from properly-lived Christian lives. It could be argued that, just as people can watch TV and listen to music for physical and mental refreshment, Christians can engage in ecstatic phenomena for spiritual refreshment. But supporters of the 'Blessing' are reluctant to say that. Such arguments are incompatible with the way they wish to present the 'Blessing'. If it were like TV or music, then the 'Blessing' would be something under our control, a kind of spiritual resource. Proponents insist, however, on seeing it as a move of the sovereign God; something which the Holy Spirit *does to us*, not something which is under our control. For them, God is the direct cause of the 'Blessing's' ecstatic experiences. It is the Holy Spirit who is bouncing people up and down, jerking them, making them fall to the ground, and so on.

Advocates of the 'Blessing' see it as a renewing work of the Lord, the beginning of the 'fourth wave' of the Spirit in this century. Stibbe says,

131

> Above all, I believe, we need to see that there is a fourth wave coming. This wave—it seems to me—will be something quite glorious.[6]

This kind of excitement is heightened by our culture's tendency for 'hype'.

'Hype'

'Hype' is something from which Christians are not immune. Indeed, the charismatic section of the church in particular has heard seemingly endless 'hyped' claims. For example, some claim to have dramatic healing ministries, without ever backing up their claims with medical documentation. I am not trying to say that miraculous healing does not happen. However, the church is infected by 'over-hyped' claims about it. Mark Stibbe recognises this problem. He tells of a poster he saw recently which advertised:

BRITAIN'S TOP HEALING MINISTRY

Amazing healings of arthritis, depression, fears, blood disorders, Parkinson's disease, scores of other diseases … Sticks and crutches often discarded in Rev. X's meetings. Lives have been changed by the power of God. The blind have seen … The deaf have heard … The lame and crippled have walked after prayers in these services …

INCURABLE PEOPLE GET CURED!
Thousands of sick people flock to his services!
Everyone gets personal attention!

One of the most successful and powerful gifts of healing in the world today![7]

Stibbe rightly states that this sort of thing does not glorify God but glorifies only the minister. Yet that is not the only problem. What Stibbe does not point out is that hype *works* in our culture. The secular world knows that in order to attract the attention of the media—and through them ordinary people—hyped-up claims have to be made. The situation is often little different with the Christian world.

Perhaps most significant are the claims that such and such an event will be one to change the world, that next year will be *the* year for world mission, that such and such a city or nation will soon be converted to Christ, and so on. With the year 2000AD approaching, and the accompanying heightened excitement about the 'end times', it was almost inevitable that many people would see the 'Toronto Blessing' as a work which will lead to Revival, and very possibly the final Revival, the one which will herald the return of Jesus Christ.

All these factors have made it virtually impossible for people involved in the 'Blessing' to understand it as anything other than a direct work of God. In my view, however, there is a much better way to understand it. I believe that we must resist the hype and be prepared to adopt a different perspective.

'Spiritual' Experiment

To most observers, it is clear that the majority of people who undergo 'Blessing' experiences are not deliberately manufacturing them. Something really does happen to them, something which can have physical, emotional and mental dimensions. Sometimes the experience is entirely physical: a person may find herself shaking uncontrollably, for example, while all the time feeling as though she is just observing with her mind what is happening. Sometimes the experience seems to involve both physical and emotional dimensions: a person may find himself laughing uncontrollably and at the same time be overcome with feelings of happiness. And sometimes the time, the experience seems to involve physical, emotional and mental dimensions. The mental dimension will tend to be in line with what is happening to the person physically and emotionally: so a person who is laughing and feeling happy might also come to believe that God is telling her he rejoices over her.

Two terms are helpful here: 'altered states of consciousness' and 'ecstatic experience'. These terms are used by many proponents of the 'Blessing', so there should be no objection to my using them. When the phenomena are described in this neutral way, we are quickly reminded of other similar phenomena to be found in the world. Indeed, some people who have received 'Blessing' experiences have noticed this. R.T. Kendall, for instance, recalls what happened to him:

> Now I once had an operation and was given sodium pentathol to put me to sleep. As Sandy prayed over me, I felt the same sense of relaxation. Though I didn't go to sleep, I found myself slumping forwards and I was helped to the floor.[8]

Many of the descriptions Christians have offered of their experiences sound very like what can be experienced at 'raves'. I was struck by this fact when I watched a Channel 4 *Equinox* programme in Autumn 1994, called 'Rave New World'. Mark Stibbe saw the same programme, and said this about it:

> [T]he point was made that hundreds of thousands of people today are pursuing happiness, and finding it in a techno trip comprising technology, dance, music and drugs. This heady mixture has created a rave culture in which Ecstasy has become a key stimulant. At airport hangars, clubs and warehouses, young people come and dance all night to music

with virtually no lyrics, and whose repetitive rhythms pound the ears with up to 180 beats per minute.[9]

Some of those participating in raves were asked by *Equinox* to describe their experience. These are the responses Stibbe records:

'There was just this massive rush of, to me, happiness, because there was a genuine brilliant atmosphere in the club and everybody was basically feeding off each other.'

'All of a sudden I got this huge whoosh running through my body and out of it, sort of thing—don't know where it went—a huge energy force almost.'

'And this would just build up and the whole crowd would just be like going along with it and becoming more and more frantic until you did actually feel as if you were slightly losing control.'

'It hits you and it bombards you and it breaks down any of those barriers between us. The rhythm just grabs hold of you.'

'I actually came away from that thinking: I have just had the best night of my life, and I have really thought I have never had a better time. It was just the happiest.'[10]

To other people, what happens in the 'Toronto Blessing' sounds similar to what goes on in some Hindu religious celebrations. Ram Gidoomal, trustee of Oasis Trust and Chair of both Christmas Cracker and South Asian Concern, says,

As a child, when I was a Hindu, we went to a temple in Nairobi—where my family had emigrated. I have vivid memories of the priests shaking incredibly violently. Some of them had very long hair, and I remember the scene of hair waving backwards and

> forwards. They performed demented dances—a little like the cossack style of dancing—and shaking like men possessed ...
>
> If you go around to Hindu temples, monuments and shrines, you will find this kind of possession. In the middle of a ceremony, someone will go into a frenzied trance. It's just like you read about the prophets in parts of the Old Testament. The point I am trying to make is that these things happen outside the Church; so if someone says—when it happens in a church—that it must be of God, it doesn't necessarily follow.[11]

To a lot of Christians, mention of 'possession' in the context of Hindu worship raises the possibility of demonic influence. When they see or hear of ecstatic-type happenings in other religions, they tend to assign them to demonic influence. In the past (even the very recent past), they have also tended to assign ecstatic experience in a church context to the demonic. It has been pointed out that in the early 1980s, when John Wimber brought his ministry to Britain, such things as severe jerking and roaring would have been blamed on demon possession.

Indeed, the majority of Christians who are involved in the 'Blessing' share a world-view in which occurrences that appear to be in the 'spiritual realm' come from either the Holy Spirit or a demonic spirit or perhaps 'the flesh'. By 'the flesh' they tend to mean the conscious 'self'. With this world-view in place, once they are satisfied that they are not consciously inducing experiences, they have the choice between assigning them either to the Holy Spirit or to demons.

The 'Blessing' occurs within an explicitly Christian setting—in churches which seek to give Jesus Christ the central place. It tends to take place in a worshipful atmosphere. The majority of those involved have good motives, seek to be obedient to their Lord, look for his glory, and so on. For these kinds of reasons, they conclude their experiences have not been caused by demons. With that option ruled out, the only one left is that they are caused by the Holy Spirit.

An good example of this kind of thinking is found on a Toronto Vineyard audio tape of a pastors' meeting question-and-answer session. During the session, somebody asked John Arnott about the meaning of the animal noises phenomena, phenomena that are particularly problematic for many Christians. He replied as follows:

> All of the animal sounds are really interesting—a challenging question. Our official answer is, we don't know why people do that—[crowd laughter]. If you eliminate the possibilities, it's either demonic, or it's the flesh, or it's the Holy Spirit. Those are the three options, I think—right? So assuming it's the Holy Spirit, then what could He possibly be doing? And therefore, we see it as a prophetic message of some point ...[12]

This is a clear example of a major leader (if not *the* major leader) of the 'Blessing' applying 'logic' in a way which binds Christians to the conclusion that their experiences are given directly by God, even when the content of the experiences would normally lead them to conclude otherwise. In my view, Christians involved in the 'Toronto Blessing' are right to think that their experiences are not demonic. But their conclusion that they must therefore be from the Holy Spirit does not follow.

Possible Causes

Patrick Dixon is a medical doctor who strongly supports the 'Toronto Blessing', and who has made popular the description of what is going on as 'altered states of consciousness' (ASCs). This term is used by medical doctors to describe one of the three states of consciousness possible for human beings. Dixon says, 'we need to recognise that there are three conscious states we enjoy: normal waking, sleeping, and a third altered state of waking, a day-dreaming, trance-like, detached, "other" mode'.[13] He thinks that in the 'Blessing' the Holy Spirit induces these ASCs—though he does not say how he can tell this. He then says some other significant things:

> Studies have been made of ASCs, as they are not limited to Christian experience. In an ASC people often feel detached from what is going on, they feel strange sensations, and see unusual things. There is often a feeling of remarkable spiritual insight, a sublime experience beyond definition or description, a feeling of oneness with God.[14]

Notice that ASCs 'are not limited to Christian experience'. Though he does not mention raves, I have no doubt that Dixon would agree that rave experiences can be described as ASCs. Rave experiences are physically and sometimes medically induced. The drug Ecstasy is taken by some (though not all), to heighten a state of euphoria in the brain that comes from the long periods of dancing in an environment of loud repetitive rhythms and psychedelic lighting.

Dixon notes a number of other things that can bring on ASCs:

> Fasting does for a start. Food deprivation forces the body to burn fat rather than carbohydrate ... The brain partly shuts down.

... [T]he person taking LSD, or using Eastern meditation techniques, or the hostage left in solitary confinement in a dark cell, may report temporal disorientation and a spiritual experience of some kind ...[15]

It seems beyond doubt, therefore, that a good many seemingly spiritual experiences are directly caused neither by demonic spirits nor by the Holy Spirit. Rather, they have what might be considered more mundane causes. This has to raise the possibility that many 'Blessing' experiences are not caused by the Holy Spirit. Exactly what the cause might be is not clear. Some people have raised the possibilities of mass hysteria and mass hypnosis, but I agree with Patrick Dixon and others, that these are not satisfactory explanations. None of the many 'Blessing' meetings I have attended have been marked by hysteria or hypnosis. It seems more likely that a combination of factors is involved.

When the 'Blessing' first came to my church in 1994, meetings were marked by considerable, but controlled, expectation and excitement. This was built up as a meeting progressed (though certainly not to an hysterical level) by testimonies of those who had already 'received', and by the meeting leader, who would talk about the 'great things God was doing'. When the part of the meeting came that was to be a 'Blessing' time, there were a good number of people who very much wanted to 'receive', and who were excited and rather nervous. At that point they were encouraged to stand still, with their eyes closed and their hands raised in front of them. Others who had already 'received' moved around the room, praying, gesturing with waving movements and often exhibiting the phenomena that they had previously received. Those who wanted to 'receive' were encouraged not to analyse or to pray. Rather, they were to relax and receive. They remained that way for long periods of time, until something happened or they gave up.

These are ideal conditions both for strange things to start happening to people physically, and for their minds to go into ASCs. If a person stands still for long enough, with their hands raised and their eyes shut, they may well begin to feel their fingers trembling or their bodies swaying. If they do not concentrate on stopping these things, but instead 'relax and receive', then the physical effects may well increase, to the point of vigorous shaking or falling down.

If a person is excited and nervous, and is asked to stand still with their eyes closed and hands raised, and they know that others are intently praying for them, and they hear strange things going on around them, then the tension within will build to a high pitch. The tension finds release in nervous laughter. Once the laughter has begun, it can easily carry over into ecstatic laughter and from there into ASCs. This is particularly so when a person is seeking an 'experience'. Weeping can occur in a similar manner. Once ecstatic experiences and ASCs have been achieved by a person, it is easier for them to occur again. This is the same with all such phenomena. From Christian meditation to yogic trances to Hindu possession, people who practice these things become increasingly adept at them.

Consequently, as the meetings continued at my church, phenomena occurred earlier and earlier in the meetings, so much so that during normal Sunday services people were trembling or laughing or breathing heavily right from the beginning of worship. It was common for times of quiet prayer and the sermon to be punctuated by people falling to the ground. As far as I could see, the people who did these things were always those who had 'received' in previous meetings. It could happen to them earlier because they were 'practised' at it, though I am sure that they did not think of it in this way. By contrast, those who had not yet 'received' needed the part of the meeting that was geared to 'receiving' in order to achieve their 'breakthrough'.

It would be pointless for me to go through all of the phenomena explaining how I think they come about. I do not have precise explanations for them all and, in any case, I do not possess the necessary sociological, psychological or physiological tools. Nonetheless, this does not affect my key point, which is that agreement that the 'Blessing' phenomena are not demonic does not force us to conclude they are caused by the Holy Spirit. They can be explained perfectly adequately by 'this-world' causes.

Conclusion

At this point it is worth setting out the claims I have sought to refute thus far:

1. The 'Toronto Blessing' is 'biblical'. I showed in Chapter 2 why this claim cannot be sustained in the senses of being either found in or predicted by the Bible. In Chapter 3, I explained why the category of 'non-biblical' does not help.

2. The so-called 'fruit' prove that the 'Blessing' is 'of God'. I showed in Chapter 4 that, plausible though it may sound, this is not a Christian way of evaluating movements, ministries or phenomena.

3. The 'Blessing' can be described as 'directly caused by God'. I have shown in this Chapter that the strange nature of the 'Blessing' does not mean that it is 'of God' in the sense of being 'directly caused by him'.

It is important to be clear that these negative conclusions still leave room for the possibility that the kind of experiences to be had in the 'Toronto Blessing' might be legitimate things for Christians to engage in in some circumstances. I believe that in the 'Toronto Blessing' a great many Christians have discovered another dimension to human existence, a dimension which is often (though mistakenly) described as 'spiritual'. It is a dimension which previously seemed to be cut off from ordinary people and of which they were perhaps afraid. Now, however, they have begun to 'experiment' with it, and have found it exciting and enjoyable. In the next Chapter I will expand on this hypothesis and begin to explore the question of how far (if at all) their experiences might be legitimate Christian ones.

NOTES

1. *Times of Refreshing* (London: Marshall Pickering, 1995), p. 72.
2. Ibid, pp. 84-85.
3. See *Times of Refreshing*, pp. 174, 178-80.
4. Ibid, p. 178.
5. Idem.
6. *Times of Refreshing*, p. 29
7. Ibid, p155
8. *A Breath of Fresh Air* (Guildford: Eagle, 1994), p. 219.
9. *Times of Refreshing*, p. 76.
10. Ibid, pp. 76-77.
11. *A Breath of Fresh Air*, p. 176.
12. The tape is dated October 19, 1994.
13. P. Dixon, 'Signs of Revival?', in 'Prayer & Revival', in *Alpha* magazine (December, 1994), p. 4.
14. 'Signs of Revival?', p. 4.
15. Idem.

CHAPTER 8

Is it ASC Exploration?

In Chapter 6, I mentioned journalist Mick Brown's visit to Toronto Airport Vineyard. I related his description of how he had a 'Blessing' experience, falling over and laughing ecstatically in one meeting. This happened in a Christian setting, but his experience cannot properly be described as 'Christian'. Interestingly, Brown interprets his experience as being similar to an experience he had at the hands of an Indian woman known as an avatar. An avatar is believed by some Hindus to be an incarnation of the divine feminine principle. It is worth repeating his description of the experience:

> What it actually involved was her taking my head in her hands for about a minute or so, and then lifting my head up and holding my gaze for another minute or so. The immediate effect was an extreme warmth on my face, a burning sensation, which lasted for a few hours afterwards. But the immediate result was that I felt mentally excited, but bemused and bewildered at the same time, trying to make sense of it, trying to rationalise it.
>
> The following day I felt positively exhilarated, absolutely on top of the world, and very beneficent to those around me. The normal day-to-day perception of life, for example, is a feeling of separateness and that had evaporated.
>
> (I remember travelling on the London Underground wanting to reach across to the person opposite and grasp him by the shoulders and say: 'Isn't it wonderful?' Of course, I did not do that. I

restrained myself.) The feeling of euphoria lasted for
two or three days.

I've spoken to other people who have [undergone
the same experience with this woman], several of
whom said that their lives had changed in quite
fundamental ways as a result ... [One woman had
previously] been rather insular, and was not
someone that people would necessarily turn to, [but]
as a result of those experiences she gradually began
to feel in herself a sense that she was more
expansive to the world, and suddenly, without any
reason, people started to turn to her more for advice,
to lean on her. It was as if the more strength she had
in herself, the more she could draw on this reservoir
of strength she felt she had found.

I did not have that kind of long-term consequence. Nor did I have any long-term conse-quence
from the 'Toronto Blessing'. What happened was that
I fell down laughing, as I described, and was on the
floor for about ten minutes. I got up rather dazed but
perfectly happy and relaxed.[1]

Brown's experience in Toronto and his experience with
the avatar sound very similar. I will return to that similarity in
a moment, but the key thing to realise here is that, in
Toronto, Brown experienced the same thing as Christians
have experienced there, yet he did not interpret it in a
Christian manner. For Brown, it was not a Christian
experience. How interpretation of an experience works can
be made clearer by returning to what Patrick Dixon says
about 'altered states of consciousness' (ASCs). He makes the
point that an ASC can happen to anybody and that it does not
automatically bring an experience of the living God:

An ASC strips us away from the overwhelmingly
immediate world around us. An ASC does not bring
us into the presence of God, only repentance and
faith can do that ...

Dixon's next words need to be questioned. He says that, though an ASC does not bring us into the presence of God, 'it does make us aware of a presence to be brought into'.[2] This needs to be questioned because, in practice, it often does not work out that way. Some Christians who have had 'Blessing' experiences have said that the experiences simply made them feel good (or, occasionally, bad) and that nothing else happened. As Dixon himself says,

> the person taking LSD, or using Eastern meditation techniques, or the hostage left in solitary confinement in a dark cell, may report temporal disorientation and a spiritual experience of some kind, but not necessarily a relationship with God as Father.[3]

I do not believe that ASCs (or 'ecstatic experiences') make us aware of a presence to be brought into. The experience in itself tells us nothing. Rather, we 'tell' ourselves (though unconsciously) what we think the experience ought to be. If we are Buddhists we will tell ourselves one thing, if we are Hindus another, and if we are Christians still another. This is not necessarily wrong, it is simply the way things are. It is the way spirituality works. When, as a Christian, I look up to the stars at night, I 'see' the wonder of their Creator: but an atheist scientist may look up and 'see' only the wonder of scientific processes, or perhaps only the wonder of the stars themselves. What *is* wrong is when we come to believe that ASCs are something they are not, namely, direct experiences of God.

I will expand on this later, but in order to do so I need first to set out my own hypothesis of what is going on.

The Hypothesis

An altered state of consciousness is, obviously enough, not a physical thing. Rather, it would seem to be something which goes on in our mental processes. Nevertheless, it seems clear that it can, and often does, have physical effects. This is similar to what can happen when we dream. When we dream, there quite often are physical effects, ranging from small things such as twitching to activities like sleep-walking.

An ASC is not a dream (because the person is not asleep), but it is very similar. The conscious self is somewhat 'disengaged' from the physical body, and so the body, free from conscious control begins to do unusual things. Here is a description of the experience of somebody who felt 'disengaged' during his experience in Toronto:

> I was introduced to Luke ... who had been shaking in the Spirit, and asked him how it had felt. *He described feeling like an onlooker*, bemused at how his own body was behaving. Above all though, he said, it had felt like an awesome 'hit' with some potent spiritual narcotic. He was high as a kite.[4]

When conscious control is disengaged, perhaps most commonly the body simply falls over, since the conscious self is no longer keeping it upright. But there are other possibilities. It may become 'locked' in one position. Or perhaps, if the person was trembling slightly before the conscious self became disengaged, the body might simply continue to tremble, and even magnify the trembling to an alarming extent. Or perhaps, if the person was beforehand inclined to laugh for some reason, once conscious control is removed he or she will laugh ecstatically. (It is interesting to note that the Toronto Airport Fellowship's meetings are known particularly for the phenomenon of ecstatic laughter, and at the same time for their happy, excited atmosphere.)

When conscious control is re-engaged, by the way, sometimes the strange phenomena are known to continue. For example, quite a number of people have been seen to continue to jerk bodily at random intervals over days and weeks, even while they are going about everyday tasks. Some people feel that this can be explained only as work of the Holy Spirit. They appear to think that, for some reason, the Holy Spirit apparently at random moments chooses to violently jerk people. In my view, the fact that a person's consciousness is no longer disengaged does not mean that the physical effects of the disengagement cannot continue.

To re-cap: in the 'Toronto Blessing' we see three main factors combining to cause the proliferation of strange physical phenomena. First, there are mental causes, such as expectation and nervous excitement, which I described in the previous Chapter. We should notice, in addition, that the majority of people involved desire an experience (even though they may also be nervous, at least the first time, about what will happen to them). It is not, therefore, a case of them being triggered into an ASC against their will. Indeed, the language of 'relaxing and receiving' (this is invariably the dominant terminology of 'Blessing' times) actively encourages people to disengage their conscious thoughts to some extent, and most are happy to do that.

Second, there are physical causes, such as standing still with eyes closed for long periods, which I also described in the previous Chapter. These two factors, mental and physical, often are enough to trigger people into altered states of consciousness. Once in ASCs, strange physical phenomena proliferate. So the third and most important factor behind the physical phenomena is the ASC itself.

These three factors provide adequate explanation of the strange physical phenomena we see in the 'Toronto Blessing'. It is therefore my conclusion that there is no need to invoke either the Holy Spirit or demons to explain them. The hypothesis is admittedly a rather rudimentary one. No doubt it could be refined and added to in a number of ways. But, I believe, in its broad outline it is adequate. What we need to consider now are the spiritual implications of the hypothesis.

Spiritual Implications

In the secular world, 'spiritual experience' is often thought of as any experience which does not have a physical cause. Christians ought not to make this mistake (though they often do). For the Christian, the word 'spiritual' means 'of or relating to the Spirit of God'. Since the Holy Spirit can be involved in all areas of our life, including the physical, this means that all areas of life have the potential to be 'spiritual'. At the same time, however, it means that we should not call something 'spiritual' simply because the secular world would call it 'spiritual'. Nor should we call something 'spiritual' simply because it takes place within a Christian context and we cannot see its cause. This is a mistake that has been made with the 'Toronto Blessing'. Christians have experienced in themselves—and seen in others—things which actually have natural causes but which they have assumed to be 'spiritual'. In effect, without realising it, Christians involved in the 'Blessing' have been participating in a mass exploration of altered states of consciousness. Hence the title of this Chapter—"Is it ASC exploration".

In the 'Toronto Blessing' people have discovered a new realm of human experience and they have entered it with almost reckless abandon. To use Mark Stibbe's term, 'ecstatic experience' has become acceptable to ordinary Christians. They have warmly welcomed it. No doubt a sociologist would be able to explain why so many Christians have been prepared to do this, but that is beyond the scope of this book.

Damage

If I am right, then a great number of Christians have jumped into one thing thinking that it was something else. Does that mean they that have been damaged? I think the answer is, 'It depends'.

The first point to make is that, since the realm of ASCs is part of created reality—part of the natural world—essentially it is good. All of God's creation is good, including those parts about which we know little. Thus exploration of this realm does not have to lead to damage, and perhaps may do good. Indeed, I would guess that, since most of the 'Blessing' experiences are to be had within the context of groups of loving people who wish only the best for others, many of the effects will have been positive. What is more, since these are Christian groups, groups that believe in the Lordship of Jesus and the goodness of God, it is entirely possible (though we have no way of knowing) that the Holy Spirit has been at work protecting people from damage. Certainly, the majority of reports about 'Blessing' meetings (whether in Toronto or elsewhere) speak of a 'good' atmosphere. Moreover, the majority of reports about actual experiences seem to involve the person having 'good feelings'.

Nevertheless, there are also reports of meetings taking place which have had a bad atmosphere; and some people have reported bad effects from their involvement. Therefore, it is naïve to think that nobody will have suffered at the subconscious level. In the physical and conscious-mental areas there is no doubt that some damage has been done. Physically, there have been people who have broken and sprained various parts of their bodies as they have exhibited physical phenomena. At my church, in the early weeks of the 'Blessing', one man badly bruised his ribs from falling over too often, while one woman broke her wrist, again from falling over. Such things are relatively trivial compared with some of the mental damage. A lot of people who have wanted to be 'Blessed' but have received nothing have, rightly or wrongly, concluded that there is something wrong with them. They have felt left out and rejected, both by other Christians and by God. Other people have 'received' something, but have been only confused and disturbed by what has happened to them.

This is a particular danger to those Christians who suffer depression or are already mentally disturbed. Many such people are particularly prone to look for 'quick fixes' for their problems. They will very readily give themselves over to strange experiences. Having done so, they may well, in the euphoria of the moment, think that their problems have been solved (and testify to that effect). But usually this is not the case, and they end up more depressed or disturbed than they were before. A similar sort of process can happen with people that are in need of physical healing.

One way of dealing with such problems and limiting the damage is for proper long-term pastoral counselling to take place in churches. Unfortunately, the phenomena have come on such a scale and at such a pace that only a tiny proportion of the necessary counselling could be possible. This is exacerbated by the fact that much of the 'Blessing' takes place in the kind of 'centres' I described earlier. People visit these 'centres' from elsewhere. They may have a very intense experience, yet they can often expect at best only a few words at the end of the meeting from one of the ministry team. For many people, that will be completely inadequate.

For these reasons, while the 'Toronto Blessing' may have done good to some people, perhaps in terms of emotional release, renewed excitement about life, and so on, it will have damaged others. Of course, the nature of the case is that the majority of those who have been damaged will keep quiet, while the majority of those who have received something positive will shout about it.

There is, however, another area of damage that is highly significant. Namely, that of people's intellectual understanding of the Christian faith, or 'theology'. The fact of the matter is that, if I am right, a very large number of Christians have been led into error about a number of things. In particular, they have been caused to think that naturally-generated phenomena are actually 'manifestations of the Holy Spirit', and that such 'manifestations' are expressive of true Christian spirituality. They have also been caused to believe that such hard won things as patience, love, humility (the fruit of the Holy Spirit, in other words) can come to them easily, by the simple act of engaging in the phenomena. I will return to this matter later, but for now I simply want to indicate that the beliefs and theology of ordinary Christians is an area in which considerable damage has been done.

Spirituality

Despite all this, I do not think that it is necessary to be entirely negative about what people have experienced. I have already made it clear that I am open to the possibility that some good things have happened at people's subconscious and emotional levels. In addition I also think that it is possible to affirm the explicitly Christian nature of many peoples' experiences. What I mean is best approached by describing further the concept of Christian spirituality.

I noted earlier that the word 'spiritual' can be applied to every area of created reality. Indeed, while at the moment human sin tends to make much of the world 'unspiritual', a time will come when the Lordship of Christ is fully realised throughout all creation. At that time, when Christ comes again, the whole of existence will be 'spiritual'. Christian spirituality has to do with moving towards that time by the power of the Holy Spirit. Thus, Christian spirituality has to do with our involvement in such things as art, ecology, the economy, even sport. Christian spirituality has to do with bringing the Lordship of Christ to bear in practical ways on these areas. James M. Houston, Professor of Spiritual Theology at Regent College, Vancouver, puts it this way:

> What we as Christians need to recognize is that spirituality, as it deals with all of Christian life before God, should be understood as the application of Christian principles to everyday life ... I see a need for all informed Christians to practice their faith in an integrated life.
>
> The practice of Christian faith is Christian spirituality. It is the experience of the reality of God in all aspects of our lives, as we relate to the world authentically and with understanding.[5]

I think it is fair to say that charismatic Christians are particularly strong at this in certain areas, while being quite weak in others. We are weak in what might be called the public, shared aspects of life, the areas that we share with the secular world. This is best explained by consideration of something that is peculiar to the modern, Western world, namely, industrial, capitalist-run society. Industrial capitalism has shaped our lives in a number of important ways. Most important for our topic is that through industrial capitalism,

> social life came to be divided into public and private spheres. The rational organization of productivity through the factory system required the concentration of human labor in a single location, outside of the home. Where work and domesticity had been fused and interdependent, now they were sundered. The 'public' sphere of wage earning would become ... increasingly separated from the 'private' realm of kinship, family, and friendship.[6]

The result of this and a number of other features of modernity has been that, whereas in the past religion played a dominant role in society, it tends now to be marginalised; whereas religious institutions used to dominate political and social life, secular institutions now hold sway. There has been a corresponding marginalisation of religion,

> in the lives of individual believers, where faith commitments become relegated to the private dimensions of family life and identity formation. In the public dimensions of the individual's life, faith is seemingly irrelevant to the nature and conduct of business. There is, then, a structural explanation for the common complaint about 'the Sunday believer'.[7]

We are all subject to this pressure. We are all part of the modern world and we cannot escape it. The pressure is on for us to give up our faith entirely or, failing that, to confine our faith to the 'private' realm. Consequently, we have often failed to apply Christian principles in the workplace, in politics and in social action. I do not mean that we have failed entirely in these areas, but we have often struggled to make any real difference. Our Christian spirituality has all too often made little impact on the modern world.

However, we have been particularly strong in the private, interior areas of life. ('Private', by the way, includes the parts of our life we share with others who have the same 'private' interests. It includes, therefore, our church life.) While many people have given up their religion entirely, charismatics have found resources which enable them to continue. This is because, as charismatics, we are especially aware of the belief that the Holy Spirit is within us. Most charismatics speak in tongues, while many prophesy and display other gifts of the Spirit. These things make us peculiarly confident that God is personally involved in our lives.

Charismatic Christians have become especially good, therefore, at 'reading God into' their experiences. In terms of Christian spirituality this is entirely proper. We should believe that God is involved in everything we do, even the most mundane things. But this 'reading in' has its down side. Charismatic Christians are well known for their tendency to translate almost every feeling, random thought, dream and coincidence into a message from God. In consequence, we are often unable to see projects through to completion with any consistency, tend to be up and down in our faith, and are often perceived by others as arrogant (as thinking that we have a special 'hotline' to God).

The point is that, although all Christians tend (rightly) to interpret their experiences in a 'God-centred' way, charismatic Christians often over-interpret them. In the 'private' realm of life in particular, they have a highly proactive spirituality. What they look for especially are things for which they cannot see a cause. During worship, a random thought or image might come into their heads, and seeing no cause (or perhaps wanting to see no cause), they interpret it as a 'prophecy' or 'vision' or 'word of knowledge'. During their ordinary lives they may be faced with a choice, for example, about career selection. They will often make their choice based on a 'feeling' which they think God has given them.

It would take another book to go into the rights and wrongs of all this. But for the moment I simply want to point out its significance for what has happened with the 'Toronto Blessing'. I believe that the majority of the experiences which can be had are, in and of themselves, spiritually neutral, since they are experiences of a part of 'the natural'. But charismatic Christians tend to interpret them in a way similar to the way they tend to interpret feelings and dreams. Because they cannot see the cause of the experience, they conclude that it is from God, and that it has some special meaning for them.

This is not necessarily bad. If somebody has an experience which gives them some good feelings, and they interpret it as indicating God's love for and joy over them, then I would say that that is a good thing. Indeed, the report of a 'Blessing' experience set out in Mark Stibbe's book, which testifies, for example, to 'the healing love of God the Father, the saving grace of God the Son, and the awesome power of God the Holy Spirit',[8] does sound thoroughly Christian. In this sense, it is possible to call the experience a Christian one. But it is a Christian experience because the one testifying already has the Holy Spirit in her enabling her to interpret the experience in a Christian way, not because the Holy Spirit actually caused the experience. A parallel can be drawn with the kind of experience a Christian might have while out walking in a beautiful mountain valley. Because we have the Holy Spirit in us, we are able to interpret such beauty as being expressive of the love, power and beauty of our Creator. We might even talk of such an experience as speaking to us and changing us. But in and of itself the experience is spiritually neutral: another person might go on the same walk and, while being aware of the beauty around them, not be 'spoken to' or changed.

Individuals' Experiences

The point I am making has two aspects to it. First, 'Blessing' experiences are, in and of themselves, neutral experiences which can be interpreted by those who are having them in a number of ways. The majority of those having them are charismatic Christians, and so the interpretations tend to be of the sort which usually come from charismatic Christians. Second, this means that criticism does not automatically mean a belittling of individuals' experiences.

This is important. One of the great difficulties for critics is to be confronted with an either/or choice between either affirming the experiences or criticising the 'Blessing'. I personally have found it a painful thing to be faced with such choices. I have had a number of conversations with friends who have felt that my criticisms of the 'Blessing' in general mean I am 'pooh-poohing' their particular experiences. The result tends to drive a wedge between friends.

People take criticisms of the 'Toronto Blessing' personally, partly because of the process of argument I described in earlier Chapters. Supporters of the 'Blessing' make their arguments depend heavily on individuals' experiences. Essentially, they say: the experiences are 'of

God' therefore the 'Blessing' is 'of God'. Consequently, critics have felt a need to reply that the experiences are not necessarily 'of God'. I have tried to show how the structure of the proponents' argument is wrong in the first place. If I am right, there is no need to belittle every 'Blessing' experience.

Of course, this does not mean that I will agree with everything somebody says about their experience. It will depend on the details of what they say and on what status they assign to their claims. If someone claims, for example, that the Holy Spirit made them jerk uncontrollably, I would feel that there is good reason to question their claim. If, in addition, they claimed that this helped prove that it is God who is doing the same thing to people all over the world today, I would feel the need to make my questioning public. On the other hand, I would rejoice in someone saying that they have had an experience in which they became more aware, for example, of the sovereignty of God. I would consider this to be parallel to the kind of thing I described earlier in which a person can go into the mountains and have a 'spiritual' experience. The problem would come if, on the basis of their experience, they began to think that walking in the mountains constitutes a direct experience of God. It would not be a big step from there to the founding of a movement which believed God has called all Christians to go mountain-trekking, and from there to the belief that the mountains themselves are divine.

This, in my view, is the direction in which the 'Toronto Blessing' is tending. Many people mistakenly think that 'natural' (though strange) experiences are divine. It is unlikely that things will go too far in this direction, because belief in the transcendence of God (and therefore in his distinctiveness from creation) is deeply enough ingrained in most Christians to guard against it. Nevertheless, it does seem to me that what is going on in practice in a great many churches is sending out the wrong message.

A Matter of Degree?

The Toronto Airport Fellowship itself is a good example. No matter what is said explicitly, the implicit message of what the Fellowship is doing is that the strange experiences are what matter. Meetings are held on six nights of every week so that the experiences can be had by whoever wishes to attend. Most of the time, its teaching and preaching is about the experiences. And, it is in order to receive the experiences that people travel from all over the world to visit Toronto. The implicit (albeit unintended) message of this is that what matters is 'the experiences'.

It seems to me that this situation is very different from the historical examples to which supporters of the 'Blessing' often appeal. It is true that there have been times in the past when strange phenomena have been experienced in the Christian church. Most popularly appealed to are those in the ministries of Jonathan Edwards and John Wesley. To me, more striking than the similarities is one crucial difference. Namely, not just in theory but in practice under the ministries of Wesley and Edwards, the strange phenomena were peripheral and the gospel central. The situation is reversed with the 'Toronto Blessing'.

When these two men preached, they preached the gospel; and on a few occasions some people were seen to fall down, or tremble, or break out in laughter. These things, however, were treated as peripheral. What mattered to

Edwards and to Wesley was whether people were responding in faith to the gospel. The strange phenomena tended to be treated as distractions. By contrast, in the 'Toronto Blessing' strange phenomena are central and the gospel has been sidelined.

There is no doubt that this difference is real. The question is, who has taken the better approach, leaders of the 'Blessing' or Edwards and Wesley? If I am right that the experiences are essentially 'natural' experiences, then the answer must be Edwards and Wesley. They usually did not belittle the experiences, but they did ensure that they were not a distraction from the gospel message.

It is a matter of degree, I think. What I mean can be explained by drawing a parallel with dance. In recent years dance has been introduced into a lot of churches as a form of worship. In my opinion, that is fine. Dance is a legitimate form of worship. It is possible to envisage, though, a church in which dancing took on special importance and became the central form of worship. Again, that is not necessarily wrong. But the situation might develop in which dancing became not so much a means of worship as a means of having 'spiritual' experiences. People might begin to dance in a trance-like state, and find that such dancing met all their 'spiritual needs'. People from other churches might go along and join in. They would feel that it was all right to do so because they were attending a Christian church. Such a church might eventually drop its other practices and focus purely on dancing. At some point along the way it might also drop its commitment to the gospel of Jesus Christ, though nevertheless still calling itself a Christian church.

This is what I mean by a matter of degree. A church can make something that in itself is perfectly legitimate so important that it unintentionally pushes the gospel of Jesus Christ out of the centre. It would be wrong for critics to rule out dancing completely, but it would not be wrong for them to point out when dancing has got 'out of place'. Similarly, since I see ASC exploration as a natural activity like dancing, it would be wrong for me to rule it out entirely for Christians at this stage. However, we need to recognise that we know very little about it at present. It may turn out after some time that an informed, sensible judgement will be reached that deliberate involvement in such activity is not appropriate. Whatever happens in the future, I do think that there are some very valid criticisms that need to be levelled. I will outline these in the next Chapter.

NOTES
1. From 'What Happened Next?', in *Evangelicals Now* newspaper (February, 1995), p. 8.
2. P. Dixon, 'Signs of Revival?' in 'Prayer & Revival' in *Alpha* magazine (December, 1994), p. 4.
3. Idem.
4. M. Fearon, *A Breath of Fresh Air* (Guildford: Eagle, 1994), p. 15 (my italics).
5. J.M. Houston, 'Modernity and Spirituality', in P. Sampson, V. Samuel and C. Sugden, *Faith and Modernity* (Oxford: Regnum Books, 1994), p. 182.
6. J.D. Hunter, 'What is Modernity? Historical Roots and Contemporary Features', in P. Sampson, V. Samuel and C. Sugden, *Faith and Modernity*, p. 19.
7. J.D. Hunter, 'What is Modernity? Historical Roots and Contemporary Features', pp. 24-25.
8. *Times of Refreshing* (London: Marshall Pickering, 1995), p. 43.

CHAPTER 9

Lordship, Truth and Grace

I said at the end of the last Chapter that I do not believe that ASCs or ecstatic experiences can at this stage be rejected out of hand for Christians. This does not mean that I think anything goes. The same theological principles apply to Christian involvement in this area as in any other. First and foremost, this means that if ASCs are valid for Christians, then the Lordship of Christ must be brought to bear upon them and be expressed by them. I want now to explain what this might mean in practice.

Truth

I showed in Chapter 5 that truth and genuine religious experience are tied together. Jesus Christ is the way, the truth and the life. The Holy Spirit leads us into truth. However, human beings exchange the truth for a lie (Rom. 1.25). Thanks be to God, Christians have been rescued from the terrible power of that lie. But, as Christians, we are not immune from the tendency to exchange the truth God has given us for a lie once again.

What is the lie, and what is the truth? Paul says in Rom. 1.25 that human beings have 'exchanged the truth about God for a lie and worshipped and served the creature rather than the Creator, who is blessed for ever! Amen.' The truth, then, involves knowing God, while the lie involves treating created things as though they were God. I say *the* lie, because that is what Paul literally says (he uses the Greek definite article), and because it expresses the fact that we are all prone to this. Every Christian finds at one time or another that he or she has become loyal to something other than God. All Western Christians, for example, know the temptation to make material wealth their ultimate goal.

In practice, this means that Christians who are involved in the 'Toronto Blessing' will undoubtedly be tempted to give 'spiritual' experience the central place in their lives. This temptation is there whether or not the experiences are 'of God'. The problem is exacerbated when those involved mistakenly believe that the experiences they are having are direct experiences of God. (Just as it can be a short step from walking in the mountains and 'experiencing' the majesty of God, to worshipping the mountains.)

The problem, of course, is that no matter how much church leaders might remind Christians that it is not the experience which is important, but God, in practice the experience *is* most important. And what happens in practice is what determines the beliefs and actions of most people. Most leaders know that what they say can have frighteningly little effect on people. It is what *happens* in a church that really matters.

Therefore, under the heading of 'Truth', I want to propose two steps that will help us move forward. First, churches must recognise that much of what has gone on under the name of the 'Toronto Blessing' has not been what people thought it was, namely a direct experience of the Holy Spirit. If this is not accepted, then a great number of Christians are destined to spend the rest of their lives on Earth seeking God where he is not to be found. Christian leaders should not delude themselves: this is a very real danger. The history of the many sects that have developed out of Christianity should alert them to that.

Second, there must be corresponding changes in the practice of those churches that have taken on board the 'Blessing'. Not all churches have become involved to the same extent. But a good many have thrown themselves in 'lock, stock and barrel'. These, in particular, need to change things quickly and radically if they are to remain on the main track of genuine Christianity.

There are also Christians and churches that have remained at something of a distance, preferring simply to get on with their more 'ordinary' (this is not meant pejoratively) Christianity. Such people and churches have taken the wisest approach. Yet there remains for them the question of what their attitude ought to be towards the 'Blessing'. Perhaps the commonest attitude, at least among charismatics, has been the kind which says, 'It is all right for them, but not for us (unless God makes it happen of course).'

I have a great deal of sympathy with this attitude. In many ways it is an eminently sensible line to take and, for young Christians especially, it is entirely understandable. However, mature Christians and church leaders need to consider whether it is an attitude drawn more from modernist ideas of plurality and tolerance than from Christian ideas of love and truth. Since we are all members of the body of Christ we have a duty, wherever possible, to ensure that our fellow Christians remain in the truth of God, and do not exchange it for a lie. This means that we must be prepared to graciously speak out where necessary (though also keep quiet where it is wise to do so).

In Chapter 4 I noted how much of modern Christianity is characterised by a mistaken search for 'results'. With the

'Toronto Blessing' this has been borne out in the concentration on the so-called 'fruit'. What people who are involved in the 'Blessing' have thought of as 'fruit' is not biblical 'fruit'—either the fruit of the Holy Spirit or the fruit of a person's character, their words and deeds—rather it is the modern world's 'fruit': results. The 'Toronto Blessing' has been accepted by many Christians because it is thought to get results, results that 'normal' Christianity has failed to get.

The tragedy is that the results may prove to be fleeting, and they are being had at the expense of truth. By 'at the expense of truth', I do not mean that theology and doctrine are being explicitly thrown away—the attitude towards these seems more to be one of putting them on hold for the moment. What I mean is that truth is being pushed to the edges. It is being treated like the fence of a school playground, beyond which it is not safe for the children to go and which keeps the wrong people out. But to treat truth in this manner is to marginalise it; it is to make it uninvolved with the thing that really counts, the children at play.

Truth is not merely a safety device, a fence. It should not be seen merely as setting boundaries beyond which Christians may not go. Truth is like the air the children breathe, without which they could not play at all. Truth, in other words, is indispensable for the whole of Christian existence:

> **Jesus then said to the Jews who had believed in him, 'If you continue in my word, you are truly my disciples, and you will know the truth, and the truth will make you free'** (Jn 8.32).

Trinitarian theology provides a good illustration of what I am talking about. Most Christians know that one of the axiomatic Christian beliefs is that God is three persons in one indivisible whole. I would guess the majority see this truth as functioning only as a boundary-belief, a playground fence: people who explicitly deny the Trinity have moved outside the Christian faith. For the rest, as long as they intellectually assent to it (or at least do not deny it), Trinitarian theology has very bearing on them. They can get on with their Christian lives without ever needing to think about this rather difficult concept of 'three in one'.

However, Trinitarian theology contains truths which set us free—truths which ought to have considerable impact on the life of every Christian. For example (and unfortunately I can go into this only briefly), one of the defining characteristics of the modern world is extreme individualism. Each human being is seen first and foremost as an individual, set apart from every other individual. Western society is constructed on such individualism. Society's function is taken to be to provide each individual with the opportunity to do whatever he or she wants. The only proviso is that, whatever the individual does, they must not harm others or prevent them from doing what they want. Society is geared towards creating and then satisfying the needs of the individual.

Ironically, society does just the opposite for the majority of people. The poor (by far the majority of the world's population) are exploited. They are treated as means of production, means of making cheap goods to satisfy our needs. Even the wealthy, who buy the cheap goods, find themselves isolated from each other and from nature. Though their material needs are met, their other, far more important, needs are neglected entirely. In addition, virtually all sense of common responsibility has been lost: self-interest rules the day. We are plagued by petty crime: large numbers of people no longer feel constrained by the good of others. The list could go on.

Christians are subject to these difficulties just as much as anybody else. Yet Trinitarian theology provides us with truths which can counteract them. The modern world treats human beings as isolated individuals, but Trinitarian theology enables us to understand that we are indivisibly related to each other. This is because we are made in the image of God, and God is three individual persons in one whole. Relationship is at the core of the divine reality. And since relationship is central to God's being, relationships should also be central *our* beings.

As members of the modern world, we have been taught to believe that to be human is to be an isolated individual. To be sure, modern people do think that relationships are important, but important only because they can make the individual happy. For instance, once a marriage no longer gives a person what they need, they may turn elsewhere. Many people feel little compunction at divorcing several times over. Others see marriage as outdated, and prefer to take up and end relationships as and when they wish. Friendship suffers similarly in the modern world.

Trinitarian theology can help us see that relationships are not there simply to make us happy. They are not the means to an end. Neither are they a kind of add-on, like a car or house. Rather, they are part of what makes us human. They are constitutive of our lives. And just as with the relationships within the Trinity, our relationships are not so much to be about taking as giving. They ought to be about constancy and commitment. If somebody else suffers, then in a very real sense I suffer too. These are truths which ought to change everything about us. If we come to view our relationships with other human beings as being central to our own personhood, all our priorities and ways of behaving will change. We will become free to be who we were created to be.

This is just one example of where truth can be so much more than a safety-device. As Christians, we must seek to live according to the truth, not because it will make us safe, but because it will enable us to live exciting, different lives. It will make us salt and light in the world. If we live according to the truth, we will live as God created us to live, and the effects will be wonderful.

I hope the tale is apocryphal, but I have heard it reported on more than one occasion that some church leaders have advised members of their congregations who have had doubts about the 'Blessing' not to let the truth get in the way of them 'receiving'. Whether these reports are accurate or not, they seem to be representative of something very real within the 'Blessing' movement. This ought not to surprise us. The tendency to put experience before truth (and all other values) is found throughout the modern world. It is another expression of the extreme individualism I described earlier. People throughout the Western world place the search for individual happiness, and the experiences which will bring it, above all else. You only need to watch American TV for a while to see that. The American dream—that I can be whatever I want to be—is more representative of modern ideals than many of us would like to think.

As Christians we must be different. It is not that we should be dour, unhappy people, who deny ourselves laughter and tears for fear of falling into error. Putting truth before experience does not mean the denial of experience, it means putting experience in its rightful place. If we live our lives according to the truth, we will find a richness and a depth to our experiences that was not there before. Without the truth we are captives, being led about by our own sinful desires and the pressures of the world. But the truth sets us free, free to live life as God created it to be lived and to know the joy and wonder of his good creation.

Lordship

According to Paul, the activity of the Holy Spirit causes us to confess the Lordship of Christ: 'no one can say "Jesus is Lord" except by the Holy Spirit' (1 Cor. 12.3). This is a theme which Luke takes up in Acts. Peter's first public words after being filled with the Holy Spirit are given over to demonstrating to his fellow Jews, 'that God has made him both Lord and Christ, this Jesus whom you crucified' (Acts 2.36). In Acts 4, Peter is 'filled with the Holy Spirit' (v. 8) and declares that Jesus 'is the stone which was rejected by you builders, but which has become the head of the corner. And there is salvation in no one else, for there is no other name under heaven given among men by which we must be saved' (vv. 11-12). Later in the same chapter, a number of believers were gathered together praying, 'and they were all filled with the Holy Spirit and spoke the word of God with boldness' (4.31).

The Holy Spirit is with and in Christians all of the time. It is clear, however, that there are times when he comes in special power. The charismatic movement on the whole seems to think that the distinctive marks of this special presence are visible 'manifestations', such as miracles, or healings or people falling over. It seems to me that when the Holy Spirit comes in power, the truly distinctive mark is that the Lordship of Jesus Christ is proclaimed to the world. I do not deny that miracles and other 'wonders' can happen at the same time. But the key thing, the thing which sets the Holy Spirit's work apart from any other, is that God's people are caused to proclaim the gospel. It is not proclamation of 'cheap grace', of blessings to be received. Rather, it is proclamation centred on Jesus Christ the Lord. It is indeed proclamation of good news, of salvation and hope, for these things attain their reality in the Lordship of Christ. It is because God has made Jesus to be Lord of all that we have hope of salvation.

With this in mind, what we need to ask of the 'Toronto Blessing' is whether it can truly be described as an outpouring of the Holy Spirit when this distinctive mark of the Spirit does not appear to be present. Certainly I see little evidence of it. This is not to say that the people involved never proclaim the Lordship of Christ: far from it. However, they proclaimed the Lordship of Christ before the phrase 'Toronto Blessing' ever existed. They are Christians; that is what they are called to do and should be doing. But I have seen no appreciable increase in such proclamation. If anything I would say that it has decreased. People have been drawn into meeting after meeting, reducing their opportunities for proclamation; and although testimonies play an important part in 'Blessing' meetings, the content of those testimonies is usually about what happened to the person when he or she 'received'—not proclamation of the gospel.

Of course, many proponents of the 'Blessing' are aware of this and rightly seek to encourage those involved to direct their energies outwards, in witness to the world. But this is something that is hoped for, not something that is happening. The 'Blessing' remains in the churches, and while it does so I believe it ought not to be called an outpouring of the Holy Spirit. Some argue that a move outwards will come; that at the moment the Spirit is 'refreshing' Christians who will soon move out on to the streets, and then the Revival will come. In arguing this way, they are tacitly admitting that at present the 'Blessing' is not causing people to proclaim the Lordship of Christ to the world. Since it is not happening, I believe that on these grounds too they have no right to call the 'Blessing' a move of the Spirit.

What then of the idea that, although Christians are not going out to the world, non-christians are coming into meetings and are being reached by the Spirit in this way? The idea brings to mind Paul's discussion in 1 Corinthians 14 concerning unbelievers attending meetings. We have already seen that the problem Paul is addressing in this section of 1 Corinthians is the over-valuation of the gift of tongues by the Corinthian Christians. They think that tongues are a sign of spirituality, and as a result their worship meetings are characterised by exercise of the gift almost to the exclusion of everything else (see v. 23). This is a situation which Paul considers unacceptable, and the reasons why are highly instructive. He sets them out as follows:

> *If, therefore, the whole church assembles and all speak in tongues, and outsiders or unbelievers enter, will they not say that you are mad? But if all prophesy, and an unbeliever or outsider enters, he is convicted by all, he is called to account by all, the secrets of his heart are disclosed; and so, falling on his face, he will worship God and declare that God is really among you* (1 Cor. 14.23-25).

In essence, Paul here offers two reasons for why meetings should not be 'hijacked' by the use of tongues. First, unbelievers entering the meetings will 'say that you are mad'. By 'mad', Paul does not mean exactly what we mean by the word. As Fee says, 'The response of the unbeliever to the community's collective speaking in tongues is to equate the

171

Christian gathering with the mania attending some of the mystery cults.'[1] In these cults people engaged in ecstatic phenomena, which they saw to be a kind of madness—or mania—inspired by the gods. Unbelievers, Paul says, will think that this is what is going on in the Corinthian church. The parallel with the 'Toronto Blessing' is striking. Some non-christians attending 'Blessing' meetings say, 'They are crazy.' Others see tremendous similarities with the ecstatic phenomena which occur in a lot of other religions, especially some Eastern and New Age ones.

The second reason Paul gives is perhaps even more important. It derives from a point he makes a number of times in ch. 14, namely, that tongues are unintelligible and thus are of no use to anyone except the person uttering them (see vv. 2, 4, 6). So, a meeting which is taken over by tongues is no use to the unbeliever. It will never draw the unbeliever to God and so to salvation. Much better, thinks Paul, are the intelligible gifts such as prophecy (v. 24). Prophecy can be understood by the unbeliever, and so can bring the unbeliever to a place of repentance and faith (v. 25). Again, the parallel with the 'Toronto Blessing' is striking. Many churches that have embraced the 'Blessing' have meetings which are dominated not by tongues but by strange physical phenomena which, like tongues, are unintelligible. Non-christians who attend such meetings may well engage in the phenomena themselves, they may even come back for more, but it will do them little good if there is no intelligible proclamation of the gospel.

To be fair, many 'Blessing' meetings do have intelligible elements to them. Meetings are often structured like a normal church service, with times of worship, times of prayer, a sermon, and perhaps also breaking of bread, and with the 'Blessing time' added on at the end. The other elements of the service may well provide opportunity for non-christians to be spoken to by the gospel. That is clearly to be welcomed. But it is worth noting that Paul does not just recommend that the Corinthians re-introduce other intelligible elements to their meetings. He actually goes further, requiring that, if the gift of tongues is exercised it should be used sparingly (two or at most three times, v. 27) and there must be an interpretation (v. 28), to make the tongue intelligible.

Paul's ideal seems to be that *every* element of a Christian gathering should be intelligible. This is because, as I showed earlier, Christian spirituality is centred in the mind. Christian meetings are most useful, therefore, when everything in them is directed at understanding the truths of God. To that end, even the intelligible gifts, says Paul, should be exercised in order and one at a time, 'so that all may learn and be encouraged' (v. 31). Spiritual development, Paul seems to think, comes from listening to one another as the Spirit is active in us. This is a far cry from the ideal of spiritual development espoused by the 'Blessing', in which individuals are pictured as communing with God on their own using their particular ecstatic experience. All that other Christians need do is look on and perhaps implore the Holy Spirit to 'Do more'.

Unfortunately, there is no space to go into this issue any further here, except to suggest that the 'Toronto Blessing' is a manifestation of modernist, individualist spirituality, while New Testament spirituality is thoroughly corporate—it depends not on direct experience of God, but on experience of God through each other: 'For where two or three are gathered in my name, there am I in the midst of them' (Mt. 18.20). This is not to say that individuals having direct experiences of God are not present in the New Testament—Paul on the Damascus road, for example—but these are exceptional. There is no sign that this sort of thing happened to any but a very few; and there is no sign that believers were encouraged to look for such experiences as a part of their normal Christian lives. Such experiences were never part of the corporate worship context. Rather, their corporate spirituality had its expression in love for one another and peace, and in thankfulness to God and worship. Since it is an expression of our being created in the image of God, with relationships at the core of our humanity, such corporate spirituality is not deficient, but an ideal to be aimed for:

> *And above all these put on love, which binds everything together in perfect harmony. And let the peace of Christ rule in your hearts, to which indeed you were called in the one body. And be thankful. Let the word of Christ dwell in you richly, teach and admonish one another in all wisdom, and sing psalms and hymns and spiritual songs with thankfulness in your hearts to God. And whatever you do, in word or deed, do everything in the name of the Lord Jesus, giving thanks to God the Father through him* (Col. 3.14-17).

Grace and Patience

The LORD passed before him, and proclaimed, 'The LORD, the LORD, a God merciful and gracious, slow to anger, and abounding in steadfast love and faithfulness, keeping steadfast love for thousands, forgiving iniquity and transgression and sin, but who will by no means clear the guilty, visiting the iniquity of the fathers upon the children and the children's children, to the third and the fourth generation'

(Exod. 34.6-7).

This quotation comes from the occasion of the second giving of the Covenant to Israel. Exodus 20 tells how the Covenant was made with Israel for the first time. God had wonderfully saved the Israelites from captivity in Egypt and had graciously chosen them to be the people who would live in covenant relationship with him. He would be their God, and he required, 'You shall have no other gods before me' (Exod. 20.3).

To be God's people is a wonderful privilege but, at the same time, much more is required of God's people than of anybody else. God demands that he alone be God, that we worship no other. Israel failed almost immediately. The people made a golden calf, and worshipped it and sacrificed to it (Exod. 32.8). Moses, on seeing this threw down and broke the stone tablets on which the Covenant was inscribed, symbolising their breaking of the Covenant. Three thousand men were put to death for their idolatry. But God, who is 'merciful and gracious, slow to anger, and abounding in steadfast love and faithfulness', renewed the Covenant with Israel, and new tablets of stone were made on which it was inscribed.

This incident demonstrates that God must never be taken for granted, but that he is nevertheless gracious and patient with us when we go wrong. Indeed, we see in Jesus Christ that God is gracious towards us even while we are doing wrong: 'God shows his love for us in that while we were yet sinners Christ died for us' (Rom. 5.8). When we go wrong, Jesus graciously comes to us and shows us the truth, bringing us back to the right way:

And the Word became flesh and dwelt among us, full of grace and truth; we have beheld his glory, glory as of the only Son from the Father ... And from his fullness have we all received, grace upon grace   (Jn 1.14, 16).

As God's children, God wants us to grow up to maturity, not remain as spiritual babes (see 1 Cor. 3.1). I believe this means that he gives us a good deal of leeway to go down paths that are not the wisest or best. And even when we go down those paths, he remains gracious and patient, continuing to give us good things, continuing to speak to us and help us.

It should be clear by now that I consider the 'Toronto Blessing' to be an unwise path for Christians and churches to follow. I do not consider it to be a blessing which has come from God. Nevertheless, I do believe that God's patience and grace mean that good can happen within it and good can come of it. In particular, I believe that there is still room for critics such as myself to say that some individuals' experiences within the 'Blessing' can have been good for them, and God can have been at work in them.

This is especially so with people who have become involved in the 'Blessing' for all the right reasons. Many have become involved because they trusted their leaders, and because they genuinely cannot see anything wrong with it. Given the overwhelming number of respected voices, at both local and national levels who have spoken in favour of it, this is hardly surprising. For many people, their involvement has genuinely sprung from a desire to be obedient to God.

Some of these people will have been damaged despite all their right intentions. As I outlined in Chapter 8, some have been damaged physically, others mentally, while perhaps others at the subconscious level. Again, some have benefited, perhaps through emotional release, subconscious change, and so on. I also said in Chapter 8 that I believe that a great deal of what people have taken to be God speaking to them is in fact over-interpretation of feelings and images for which they are unable to see natural causes. Nevertheless, this does not rule out the possibility that God has actually spoken to some people in and through their experiences. I rejoice that this has happened and will continue to happen. God is a loving, gracious, wonderful Father.

'Fruit' (Again)

In light of this we must return to the argument about 'fruit'. Among all the issues, this is the one which proponents return to again and again. Many church leaders seem to feel embarrassed by the strange physical phenomena, but they are prepared to live with them because of the 'fruit' that the experiences are supposed to bring. Terry Virgo, leader of the New Frontiers International group of churches, says, for example,

> I am so glad that, from the beginning, I saw substantial spiritual fruit in the lives of those affected. The immediate manifestations were so strange, but the continuing impact on people's lives has been magnificent.[2]

Perhaps the classic formulation of the idea is found in the oft-repeated comment of the Bishop of London:

> I don't mind them falling down. What I want to know is whether they are any good when they get up![3]

In almost everything I have read in support of the 'Toronto Blessing', this sort of idea is to the fore. I have shown in Chapter 4 why it is wrong to use the 'fruit argument' as a test of whether movements are of God. But, because the claim that the 'Blessing' does bring godly change is asserted so loudly and so often, we must once again briefly examine the substance of the claimed changes in people. On this occasion we will look at it from the point of view I established in Chapter 8, namely, that people are engaged, without realising it, in exploring altered states of consciousness, rather than in a move of God.

If the 'Toronto Blessing' is what I have argued it is, if it is a movement of ASC exploration, then it is something which the vast majority of Christians have not experienced before. It is something new and exciting, which many have thrown themselves into wholeheartedly. Consequently, it would be surprising if changes in people's attitudes and ideas did not follow. It would be surprising, too, if they did not also feel 'refreshed' by these new and exciting changes. I do not mean to be cynical by saying that, merely realistic.

Proponents and critics alike are agreed that the 'Toronto Blessing' requires enormous changes in people's understanding of the Christianity they are involved in. Those people who choose continued involvement must be prepared to change their ideas about many things. Furthermore, once they have experienced altered states of consciousness and physical phenomena that are completely new to them, such people will find almost all their natural psychological 'defences' against change to be considerably weakened. Since they believe that God is behind what has happened to them, they will be prepared, in the period following the experiences, to change whatever they think God wants them to change.

It would be surprising then if the 'Blessing' were not accompanied by confession of sin, repentance and change of behaviour and attitude. Such things are to be welcomed, of course. But we must be clear about what they are. They are the results of a person's change of mind. They take place because a person is psychologically brought to a position of preparedness to change, and because the person believes that

God wants them to change. This is true whether or not the person's experience was directly caused by the Holy Spirit.

This is an area in which we must be tough-minded. Repentance, confession of sin and change—where genuine—are all good. But they cannot be allowed the final say in whether the 'Toronto Blessing' is of God or not. I gave reasons in Chapter 4 for why it is not biblical to test movements in this way, but it is worth noting a few other reasons here. I would prefer not to have to do so, and to simply rejoice. Since, however, supporters of the 'Blessing' make such things into proof that it is from God, it is necessary to question their status as proof. Gerald Coates, for instance, in answer to the question, 'Where are the positive arguments that validate the "Toronto Blessing"?' says he that can tell 'story after story of the fruit of this blessing in terms of repentance, confession of sin, changes of behaviour and a godly atmosphere …'[4]

True repentance is a matter between the individual and God, a matter of which even church leaders of many years standing cannot be sure. When leaders hear members of their churches professing repentance they will rightly rejoice, but they will be wise not to make anything more of it. Repentance which comes during times of heightened excitement and emotion (which no-one can deny is what we have now), is notoriously unstable. It is similar to repentance that comes at times of fear. Once the excitement or the reason to fear has passed, many of those who repent will return to their old ways. John the Baptist, who preached 'a baptism of repentance' (Mk 1.4), said words to some of those who professed repentance which are salient here:

> **But when he saw many of the Pharisees and Sadducees coming for baptism, he said to them, 'You brood of vipers! Who**

> *warned you to flee from the wrath to come? Bear fruit that befits repentance'* (Mt. 3.7-8).

These Pharisees and Sadducees repented out of fear of 'the wrath to come', not out of sorrow for their sins. I do not mean to say that all those who profess repentance are like these Pharisees and Sadducees. No doubt there will be a mixture of true and false repentance. But what the proportion will be none of us can tell.

The difficulty is that those who already think that the 'Blessing' is a move of the Holy Spirit will expect most of the professions of repentance to be genuine (with, no doubt, a few counterfeits by which the devil will try to bring the move into disrepute), while those who think that the 'Blessing' is something else, will expect many professions of repentance to be the result of excitement and emotionalism (with, no doubt, some genuine repentance brought about by the gracious hand of God). Consequently, to those who are involved, it really does seem that the 'Blessing' is overwhelmingly bringing good things, while to those who are critical it really does seem that the 'Blessing' is in large part bringing indifferent and bad things. This is why we must be tough-minded and not allow appeals to stories of repentance and confession of sin to decide the matter. Judgements about such things are far too subjective.

Finally in this section, I would like to point out one more thing that is not surprising in the light of all the new and exciting changes Christians experience in the 'Toronto Blessing'. It is not surprising that these new and exciting changes are causing many people to feel 'refreshed' in their Christianity. The dictum, 'A change is as good as a rest' is a fairly well-worn, but it is nevertheless often true. When people feel tired, bored, even frustrated with their jobs or their lives, a change can even be better than a rest. Of course, not everyone who has had an experience was previously feeling tired, bored and frustrated, but it is clear a good many were. Mark Stibbe, for example, tells us,

> In July of 1994 I was desperate. My own spirituality was one of performance rather than reality. I was leading my church as if I was on fire for the Lord when in truth I was little more than a smouldering wick ... I had become a prey to vanity and ambition, and as a consequence was tired, anxious, and depressed. Ministry had become a burden to me ... By the summer of 1994 I was very dry spiritually, worn out physically, and pretty low emotionally.[5]

Stibbe thinks that this is typical of many. He says,

> The truth of the matter is that many of those who are experiencing refreshing from the Lord are doing so after a journey through tiredness, repentance and hunger. There are many stories being told of pastors and leaders who have reached rock bottom ...[6]

From his experience as a leader at Toronto Airport Vineyard, Guy Chevreau reaches a similar conclusion:

> In the wake of a defeated, discouraged and characteristically exhausted Christian experience, thousands of believers have returned to their 'first love' ... Thousands of desperate and burned-out pastors and spouses have received a refreshing ...[7]

There is no dispute that many people have felt refreshed by their experiences. It is entirely understandable that 'times of refreshing' has caught on as a way of describing the 'Blessing'. Yet is clear to me that this 'refreshment' is fully explained by the factors I have described, namely, 'new and exciting changes'. This does not make the 'refreshment' a bad thing in itself. But it is another example of the so-called 'fruit' about which we must be tough-minded and not allow to sway our judgement.

Conclusion

Stories of 'refreshment', repentance, confession and the like, do not alter my conviction that the 'Toronto Blessing' has been an unwise path for people and churches to follow. Where repentance is genuine, that is to be welcomed. But it does not alter the fact that the 'Blessing' is a path which can be followed only at great expense—at the cost of truth and the Lordship of Jesus Christ. Those who have taken it must seek to get on the right path quickly before the way back becomes too difficult. For some people (particularly leaders and 'experience-seekers') this will mean repentance, while for others there may be no real need to feel guilt.

God is gracious and patient. He has been gracious and patient with people as they have been involved in the 'Toronto Blessing', and, if they wish it, he will graciously and patiently provide for them a way out.

NOTES
1. G. Fee, *1 Corinthians* (NICNT; Grand Rapids, MI: Eerdmans, 1987), p. 685.
2. Terry Virgo, 'Fresh Outpourings of the Holy Spirit', in *The Impact of Toronto* (Crowborough: Monarch, 1995), pp. 25-26.
3. Quoted, for example, on the back cover of *The Impact of Toronto*.
4. This is a letter published in the *Christian Herald* newspaper (23/9/95).
5. *Times of Refreshing* (London: Marshall Pickering, 1995), pp. 139-40.
6. Ibid, p. 143.
7. *Catch the Fire* (London: Marshall Pickering, 1994), pp. 18-19.

CHAPTER 10

Conclusion

For better or worse, the 'Toronto Blessing' is with us, and seems to be here to stay. Its impact on church life has been huge. We cannot pretend that it never happened. Therefore, it is imperative we come to a proper understanding of what it is and what it is not.

In the first part of this book I described why I think it cannot be understood to be biblical, or even to produce 'fruit' that is biblical. In the second part, I set out what I think we should understand the 'Blessing' to be, namely, a mistaken exploration of altered states of consciousness—of ecstatic experience—and why it should not be understood as a movement of the Holy Spirit. This leaves a lot of questions unanswered. In particular, people who have had an experience, but who now accept my conclusions about the 'Blessing', will need to come to terms with what they have been through. That is a pastoral problem which I do not have the competence to deal with. In Appendix 2, however, I have offered what I hope are some useful theological perspectives on it. They may help those who have been involved to begin to evaluate their experiences.

In closing, I want to highlight something which will seem of less immediate importance to those involved, but which I believe is—in the long term—much more important.

The Place of the Bible

The single most important reason why the 'Toronto Blessing' has been so readily received by charismatic Christians is the removal in practice of the Bible from its place of authority in their churches. I say 'in practice' because most charismatic churches hold to the theoretical belief that the Bible is their final authority in matters of faith and action, while in practice it does not function that way. Many churches will not recognise themselves in this description, because they still have sermons which are preached from Bible texts and they still hold 'Bible-teaching' sessions. But the fact is that even when these are present, the Bible often does not function as an authority.

The reason is (and I am generalising of course: there are exceptions) most charismatic churches are not serious about the difficult, strenuous task of discovering what the Bible has to say. Rather than spend time learning principles of good exegesis and learning how to use the many tools of Bible interpretation that are available to them, their preachers and Bible teachers prefer to rely on their own innate 'spirituality' in combination with the Holy Spirit to tell them what a text means. Interest among charismatic Christians in learning the original Bible languages, Greek, Hebrew and Aramaic is minuscule; interest in hermeneutics and theology is virtually non-existent. Indeed, in many quarters, those people who do study such things, far from finding themselves in demand for what they have to offer, are regarded with considerable suspicion.

The result is that, much of the time, charismatic preachers and Bible teachers simply use Bible texts as a pretext to say what they think is right, without making any real effort to discover what the Bible itself says. At the same time, there is little serious checking by others that what is taught really does measure up to what the Bible says. Those who doubt that this is the case need only look at some of the woeful examples of Bible 'interpretation' that have been offered in support of the 'Toronto Blessing' in the few months after it came to this country.

One such interpretation that was offered of Phil. 2.12 by a nationally renowned leader in one of Britain's most popular Christian magazines.[1] Phil. 2.12 says, 'work out your salvation with fear and trembling'. So, because of the word 'trembling', the leader claimed that this verse 'gives more than sufficient evidence and endorsement' of 'Blessing' type trembling and shaking. I have explained in Appendix 1 why it does nothing of the sort. Such a renowned leader should have recognised the weakness of his interpretation and should have tried to understand what the verse is really saying. Instead, he offered similarly poor interpretations of about thirty other verses. These verses are supposed to endorse 'Blessing' type phenomena, but in fact do nothing of the kind. In addition, the editor of the magazine should have realised the woeful nature of the Bible interpretation in this article, but instead, he or she characterised it as 'a robust response to the doubters'.

The point I am making is that charismatic churches have reached a stage where such things are normal. What the Bible says has been confused with what people say on the pretext of some words in certain Bible verses. And, on the whole, the ability to distinguish between the two has been lost. Consequently, even though the Bible is often used in charismatic churches, what the Bible says is no longer the authority. This is a situation which must change if God's truth is to reign once again in his church. We have access to God's Word through the Bible, if we are prepared to do the hard work of trying to understand what it says. If we are not, then we will hear only our own voices echoed back to us from the text.

I am not advocating a return to rigid fundamentalism. One of the reasons people have moved away from biblical authority is that in the past it has been unnecessarily tied to fundamentalist views such as belief in things like the inerrancy of Scripture. Many people have rejected fundamentalism and views such as inerrancy. But the proverbial baby has been thrown out with the bath water: they have also rejected such things as serious exegesis and hermeneutics, which fundamentalists rightly hold dear.

It is crucial that those of us who do take the Bible's authority seriously, demonstrate in practice that this does not mean a rigid, dry, uninteresting faith. It is also important that we show why taking the Bible's authority seriously does not mean rejection of the authority of the Holy Spirit and of the renewing life which the Spirit brings. But at the same time it is essential that we do speak out, loudly and clearly, the message that charismatic Christians must return to the authority of the Bible.

The Work of the Spirit

Much of this book has been given over to demonstrating why, on the basis of what the Bible says, I do not believe that the 'Toronto Blessing' is a work of the Holy Spirit. I would like to end, therefore, with some thoughts about what, on the basis of the Bible, a work of the Holy Spirit does look like.

Consider a passage that is often quoted in support of the 'Blessing', Ezek. 3.23:

> *I arose and went forth into the plain; and, lo, the glory of the LORD stood there, like the glory which I had seen by the river Chebar; and I fell on my face.*

Here, the prophet Ezekiel is given an extraordinary vision of God in his glory, and he falls face down on the floor (presumably expressing his fear and awe at this incredible sight). Verse 24 tells us what happened next: 'But the Spirit entered into me, and set me upon my feet; and he spoke with me' (the next verses tell us what the Spirit said). Notice the sequence: Ezekiel throws himself down, and the Spirit stands him up again (not literally, in my view, as though there is an invisible rope pulling him to his feet) and speaks to him.

I believe that this points us in the direction of an important principle, which is found throughout the Bible: God, the Holy Spirit, is not one who casts us down, rather, he is one who (metaphorically) picks us up and sets us on our feet—see also Psalm 10. A responsible, serious reading of the Bible enables us to see that the Spirit does not embarrass or humiliate God's children, but restores to us our dignity as human beings created by God (e.g. Eph. 2.1-10). He does not make us appear like fools (except in our proclamation of the 'foolishness' of the cross); instead, he restores us to our right minds (Mk 5.15).

It seems to me that the Holy Spirit portrayed in the Bible is not someone who takes our wills away from us, making us shake and jerk even if we do not want him to. Rather, he is one who gives us the will to take responsibility for all we do, enabling us to do all things in love, joy, peace, patience, kindness, goodness, faithfulness, gentleness and self-control, which are the true fruit of the Spirit (Gal. 5.22-23). These are the marks of the Spirit-filled life which the Bible witnesses to, the kind of life that God by his Spirit enables us to live. I hope and pray that God will cause this fruit, and no other, to abound in his church.

NOTES

1. Gerald Coates, '"Toronto" and Scripture', in *Renewal* magazine (No. 222; November, 1994), pp. 24-27.

APPENDIX 1

Bible Texts

Despite vigorous objections from a number of quarters, the claim still persists that the 'Toronto Blessing' is 'biblical' in the sense that the physical phenomena are found in the Bible. In this Appendix, I list every biblical text which I have seen published in support of this claim, and explain whether I think they are relevant to the 'Blessing'.

The first question I ask about these texts is whether, according to the normal rules of interpretation, the thing described in the text can properly be equated with the phenomenon currently being experienced. If it cannot, then the text cannot be used to say the 'Toronto Blessing' is biblical. In asking this question, there are a number of criteria that I have applied. They are as follows:

A. Does the language of the text in question indicate that the phenomenon it mentions is meant literally or metaphorically? For example, Josh. 14.8 contains the phrase, 'But my brethren who went up with me made the heart of the people melt'. Joshua is describing what happened when the spies returned from the Promised Land to tell the people what the land was like. Their descriptions of giants in the land made the people fearful. Joshua uses the metaphor of 'hearts melting' in order to describe their fear. This kind of poetic language is often used in the Bible, and should not be taken literally. If the context indicates that the language is metaphorical, then it should not be equated with a physical phenomenon of the 'Toronto Blessing'. If there were such a 'Blessing' phenomenon as hearts physically melting (thankfully there is not—this would result in death!), such a thing could not be equated with Josh. 14.8.

B. Does what is described actually happen to a human being? If not, it is not relevant. For example, Ps. 2.11 describes God as laughing. This has no bearing on the question of whether there is human ecstatic laughter in the Bible.

C. If what is described is meant literally and happens to a human being, does it describe something which happens involuntarily to the person? A key feature of the 'Blessing' phenomena is that, for the person having the experience, it seems to happen to them, rather than them voluntarily making it happen. If the thing described in the biblical text happens voluntarily, therefore, it cannot be equated with a 'Blessing' phenomenon. For example, if somebody voluntarily falls to the floor in a biblical text, that is not the same thing as the *involuntary* falling which accompanies the 'Toronto Blessing'.

D. If what is described does happen involuntarily, does the text offer a reason for why it happened? Is the reason other than that it was caused by God? 'Blessing' experiences are supposed in some way to be caused by God, or by being in the presence of God. If the text indicates some other reason for why the thing happened, then it cannot be equated with a 'Toronto Blessing' phenomenon.

E. Does the text actually mention the phenomenon it is being compared to? If it does not, then there is no possibility of equating the 'Blessing' phenomenon with the text. For example, Gen. 15.12 is sometimes used as support for the phenomenon of falling down. In fact it does not mention falling down, only that 'a deep sleep fell on Abram'.

F. Many of the texts are referred to for a different reason. They are not thought to be examples of what is seen in the 'Toronto Blessing', but they are thought to legitimize the phenomena in a different way. For instance, Rev. 5.5 speaks of Jesus as the Lion of the tribe of Judah. It is thought that this text lends legitimacy to the phenomenon in which people roar like lions. The idea seems to be not so much that Jesus is using peoples' mouths to roar through as that these people are roaring in order to prophetically declare that Jesus is the Lion of Judah. I will return to this issue at the end of the Appendix, but for now I need only make the point that when the text is being quoted for this reason, it does not show that a 'Blessing' phenomenon is itself 'biblical' in the sense of being present in the Bible.

A number of the texts that are often quoted refer to phenomena such as 'prophecy' and 'revelations'. It is worth pointing out that I am considering only physical phenomena, not such things as prophecy. I do not dispute that these latter are in the Bible. It is also worth noting that I do not dispute the presence of some highly unusual physical phenomena in the Bible that are caused by God—such as God putting Adam into deep sleep (Gen. 2.21). The issue is not whether strange things happen in the Bible, but whether the strange things we are seeing in the 'Toronto Blessing' happen in the Bible.

With that in mind, it is necessary to set out in some detail what the major physical phenomena of the 'Blessing' are. The descriptions I offer are drawn from what appears to happen in the majority of cases. There are other things that happen in some cases, but it would take too long to provide exhaustive descriptions. I think I have provided fair descriptions of the major features. It is these features which must be present in the biblical text if we are to say that the phenomenon is found there.

Falling—this seems to occur either by sudden relaxation, or loss of strength in the legs or by being rocked backwards or forwards by some unknown 'force'. The falling can be accompanied by many different emotions or by none at all. Often the person will just lie on the floor with no conscious thoughts of any kind, only with a feeling of peace and restfulness.

Shaking/trembling—a vigorous trembling or shaking, sometimes confined to hands and arms, sometimes spreading to other parts of the body; it can last for long periods of time. Most often it is not accompanied by any sense of fear.

Drunkenness—a loss of co-ordination over limbs and sometimes voice and mind, leading to staggering and other drunken-like phenomena. This can last for long periods of time, even going on outside of meetings.

Laughter—extended periods of 'hearty' laughter. The key feature is that it appears to have no external trigger of which the conscious mind is aware, such as someone telling a joke, or something funny happening. Instead, the laughter is perceived to have been directly caused. The person simply finds him or herself laughing. It is ecstatic laughter, as distinguished from ordinary laughter. Here is part of an account from someone who has experienced it, which seems to be fairly typical:

> I found myself swaying, and I don't remember starting. After a while I began to laugh from the depths of my gut. The bit of me that is analytical was listening and looking, wondering what was

happening; my emotions were the last part of me to be touched. I never felt that my sense of self-control was being overridden. I always felt that what was happening had not been initiated by myself, and that I could have stopped it had I wished, but I could find no reason to stop. There was deep sense of personal liberation.[1]

Weeping—extended periods of deeply-felt crying. Again, the key feature is that there appears to be no external trigger of which the conscious mind is aware. It is ecstatic weeping.

Roaring like a lion—deep, loud noises, made in the back of the throat.

Strange noises—such as barking like dogs, gobbling like turkeys, growling and moaning.

A number of other phenomena have been observed in the 'Toronto Blessing', such as 'pogo-ing', air-boxing, violent and random jerking of the torso, crawling on all fours and simulated labour pains. I have not seen attempts made to demonstrate the presence of these in the Bible, so they are not dealt with here.

In addition, mixed in with the kind of ecstatic phenomena described above, there have also been a good many other 'ordinary' phenomena. People have laughed and cried, felt afraid, felt joyful, and so on. This Appendix does not deal with such things. It deals solely with the strange, physical phenomena of the 'Blessing'.

In order to keep the Appendix to a reasonable length, I have set out my explanations in a kind of shorthand. This takes the following form:

Text reference—phenomena the text is supposed to refer to—letters of relevant criteria (**A**, **B**, **C, D**, **E** or **F**)—if necessary, short explanation of why the text fails the criteria.

Gen. 15.12—falling—**E**—Abraham falls into a deep sleep, there is no mention of him literally falling down.

Gen. 17.17—laughter—**E**—this is what would be described as 'ordinary laughter' (though, of course, it is caused by something far from ordinary: God speaking). There is no sign that it is the unusual ecstatic laughter seen in the 'Blessing', rather, God has promised something which Abraham finds absurd, so he laughs. This is not to say that ordinary laughter is not taking place in 'Blessing' meetings, even ordinary laughter that is triggered by God saying something. But it is the presence of ecstatic laughter in the Bible that is at issue here.

Gen. 18.12—laughter—**E**—see previous note.

Gen. 21.6—laughter—**E**—see Gen. 17.17 note. Here the laughter involves joy because God has done the impossible and given the aged Sarah a child.

Exod. 20.18—trembling—**E**—the verse makes it clear that there is an external cause (terrible thunder, lightning, etc.) for the people's extreme fear which in turn causes them to tremble. This is different entirely from the 'Toronto Blessing' phenomenon, which is characterised by lack of fear and which usually involves highly exaggerated motions that are not consistent with fearful trembling. This is not to say that on some occasions people might not tremble with fear in 'Blessing' meetings.

Judg. 2.4—weeping—**C E**—the angel of the Lord accuses the people of having done wrong. The people are convicted of their wrong and feel terrible remorse, which they express by weeping. There is no indication that this is 'ecstatic weeping'. Again, this is not to say that weeping as a result of conviction of wrongdoing is not taking place in 'Blessing' meetings. Where it does take place, it is to be welcomed. But it is 'ecstatic weeping' that is at issue here.

1 Sam. 1.13—drunkenness—**E**—'Eli thought Hannah was drunk'. The verse itself tells us why Eli thought this: 'As she continued praying before the LORD, Eli observed her mouth. Hannah was speaking in her heart; only her lips moved, and her voice was not heard; therefore Eli took her to be a drunken woman'. Hannah was certainly not displaying loss of co-ordination, either of limbs or mind.

1 Sam. 19.24—falling—**C E**—Saul strips off his clothes and lies naked all day and night. This is not a phenomenon that is characteristic of the 'Toronto Blessing'!

2 Chr. 5.13-14 (and its parallel, 1 Kgs 8.11) —falling—**E**—these verses come from a description of an extraordinary occasion. The building of the temple has just been completed and the ark of the covenant has brought into the holy of holies. As the worshippers begin to praise God, the Lord demonstrates his presence: according to the RSV, the temple 'was filled with a cloud so that the priests could not stand to minister because of the cloud; for the glory of the LORD filled the house of God'. The Hebrew word translated by the RSV as 'stand' is *amad*, which has a wide range of meanings that centre around the idea of continuing to do something. Therefore, the NIV, for example, translates 'the temple of the LORD was filled with a cloud, and the priests could not perform their service because of the cloud'.

A number of other versions translate similarly. This demonstrates that it should not be claimed that the text in the original Hebrew speaks specifically of falling. It speaks specifically only of the priests being unable to continue ministering, perhaps because they could not remain upright but perhaps for some other reason. In any case, the text does say that the reason for their inability to stand was the cloud itself. The text indicates that this cloud was a real visible thing, separate from the people, representing God's real glorious presence in the temple. The cloud was not, for example, only present as an internal vision or feeling of God's glory. This extraordinary event seems to me to be significantly different from any of the meetings I have ever experienced (either in person or by watching videos) in which the 'Blessing' takes place. A great number of people fall over in these meetings, but always because of some unseen, internal cause, not from response to an external, visible cloud of God's glory.

2 Chr. 34.27—weeping—**C E**—see Judg. 2.4 note.

Neh. 8.9—weeping—**C E**—see Judg. 2.4 note.

Job 8.21—laughter—**C E**—Job has been devastated by the loss of his great wealth, his children and his health. Not surprisingly he has nothing to laugh about, no reason to be happy. In this verse his friend Bildad tries to comfort him by saying that God will 'fill your mouth with laughter'. In isolation, these words may sound like a promise of ecstatic laughter. However, in the context of the book, they must mean that Bildad thinks God will restore to Job reasons for confidence and happiness, and when this happens, Job will be able to laugh again. Thus the verse is about 'ordinary' laughter, not ecstatic laughter.

Ps. 2.11—trembling and shaking—**A**—there is a particular problem with quoting this verse in support of 'Blessing'-type trembling, which is that, as a number of Bible translations mention in their margins, the Hebrew text is uncertain at this point. Therefore, its precise meaning is uncertain.

However, even if we ignore that problem, there is another. The verse's origin in a psalm should alert us to the fact that poetic language is being used here. 'Trembling' is a poetic word that emphasises the need for an attitude of reverence and even fear, just as the smashed 'potter's vessel' in v. 9 is poetic language emphasising how the proud nations will be vanquished by God and his anointed. 'Trembling' occurs again and again like this throughout the Bible.

The need to recognise metaphor and poetic language is highlighted by the fact that the words immediately following v. 11 are 'kiss His feet'. It simply is not possible to take these words literally and kiss the Lord's feet. In general, only by recognising that it is using poetic language do we properly appreciate the meaning of the psalm. Psalm 2 is about recognising the awful mightiness of God and behaving accordingly. It is not about 'Blessing'-type trembling, where most people have been reported as trembling for long periods without any feelings of fear or awe. Of course a reverent or fearful person might find their hands trembling slightly, but not whole limbs in the exaggerated, often grotesque way seen in the 'Toronto Blessing'. When people tremble in the way that sometimes does accompany fear, their trembling is usually not especially noticeable. If this sort of trembling were taking place in 'Blessing' meetings (and in some cases it may indeed be doing so), it would not be considered a strange physical phenomenon. The whole point about most of the trembling and shaking of the 'Blessing' is that it is obviously different to normal trembling and shaking. If it were not different it would not have become famous.

Ps. 65.8—laughter—**E**—this verse is about God as Creator being ultimately responsible for all the joy that is experienced by people throughout the earth. It does not speak of 'ecstatic laughter' (though, of course, it does not rule out the joy which might be received in that way).

Ps. 99.1—shaking and trembling—**B**—talks about the nations trembling and the earth shaking. As vv. 1-3 indicate, this is poetic language that expresses the need for all creation and all people to recognise in reverence that the great and holy Lord reigns over all. See note on Ps. 2.11.

Ps. 114.7—trembling—**B**—the verse is one among six verses which speak of mighty natural events (such as earthquakes) expressing the mightiness of God.

Ps. 119.120—trembling—**A**—see note for Ps. 2.11. The author is not at his desk shaking as he writes. He is merely using poetic language to express the awesome nature of his God and the need for reverence. Notice how six verses earlier (v. 114) he uses poetic language (God is described as a shield) to express security of being one of God's people.

Ps. 126.2—laughter—**E**—there is nothing to indicate this is ecstatic laughter; rather, 'ordinary' laughter and joy are meant. See Job 8.21 note.

Eccl. 3.4—laughter—**E**—see previous note.

Isa. 42.13—roaring and shouting—**B F**

Isa. 59.11—strange noises—**A D E**—the people have sinned terribly, against each other and against God. As a result, the situation within Israel is extremely bad. Verse 11 expresses poetically how the people feel in this situation.

Jer. 5.22—trembling—**A**—see note for Ps. 2.11.

Jer. 23.9—shaking—**A**—this text speaks specifically of Jeremiah's distress at the presence of false prophets in the land. Jeremiah uses poetic imagery to describe his distress. One proponent of the 'Blessing' claims that, in a way similar to what happens in the 'Blessing', 'Jeremiah is relating that what happened to him on at least one occasion involved a trembling/shaking of his bones. His wording seems to imply that he shook from the inside out. It would take a powerful force to cause his bones to quiver inside his body.'[2]

The wording should not be pushed to a literal extreme like this since the verse runs, 'My heart is broken within me, all my bones shake': if Jeremiah's heart is literally broken, then he is dead and unable to describe his experience! This is not to say that, at this time of deep emotional distress, Jeremiah did not experience some accompanying physical reaction. Sometimes, for example, people get so angry that they literally shake. But it is the anger which causes them to shake. This is very different from 'Blessing'-type shaking, which is perceived to be caused by some non-human force, and which in any case appears almost always to be accompanied by 'good feelings', not by anger and distress.

Jer. 23.9—drunkenness—**A**—see previous point.

Jer. 25.30—roaring—**B F**.

Jer. 31.9—weeping—**E**—The context shows that this is a prophecy of a wonderful time when God will bring his people back from terrible exile to the land of Israel. Presumably, 'weeping' here means tears of relief and joy. It is reasonable to say that it could be applied to the tears of joy and relief a person may have on becoming a Christian and also at later stages in their Christian life. But it is not reasonable to say that it is explicitly speaking of the involuntary and uncontrolled crying that is found in ecstatic weeping.

Ezek. 1.28—falling—**E** (and probably **C**)—is this the 'falling over' currently being experienced in the 'Toronto Blessing'? The majority of those who fall over (usually backwards, we should note), say that it is an involuntary or partially involuntary act, i.e. one which happens to them. And they feel it is caused by something strange happening in their bodies. There is no reason to think that Ezekiel experienced that here. The reason for his falling is given in the verse: he has a tremendous vision of God. The text does not give us any more detail than that, but presumably the vision filled him with awe and fear, and either he fell involuntarily to the ground or (and to me this seems more likely) his natural reaction was to cast himself voluntarily face down on the floor, as an expression of self-abasement and worship: 'And when I saw the likeness of the glory of the LORD, I fell upon my face'. The Hebrew word for falling here (*naphal*) can just as easily mean voluntarily falling to the floor as it can involuntarily. For example, when Joseph's brothers came to him in Egypt, 'they fell (*naphal*) before him to the ground' in order to express his greatness and their guilt before him (Gen. 44.14). It is worth noting that in Ezekiel the Spirit's activity is specifically associated with enabling Ezekiel to get up off the floor (2.2, 3.24, 43.5), not with making him fall down.

It is significant that the majority of the cases of 'falling down' in the Bible are occasions where a person or people are confronted by one greater than themselves (often God or an angel of God), and in response they cast themselves down in fear and worship. There is no indication in these cases that God's Spirit directly causes the falling down by doing something strange to their bodies.

Finally and most importantly, 'falling down' in the 'Toronto Blessing' seems to lack the key feature of the biblical cases, namely, some sort of vision of God. Instead, the majority seem to be in a kind of 'switched off' state in which they 'feel good', 'happy', etc.

Ezek. 3.23—falling—**E** (and probably **C**)—see previous point.

Ezek. 43.3—falling—**E** (and probably **C**)—see note on Ezek. 1.28.

Dan. 8.17—falling—**E** (and probably **C**)—see note on Ezek. 1.28. This verse tells us that Daniel is frightened by his encounter and that is why he falls (whether voluntarily or involuntarily it is again impossible to tell). Notice how, as with Ezekiel, the Spirit's activity is associated with him getting up, not falling down (v. 18)

Dan. 10.7—trembling—**E**—men tremble in fear. Again, this seems a long way from the uncontrolled shaking of limbs for no apparent reason that happens in the 'Toronto Blessing'. Most of those who report such shaking are certain that they are not doing it out of fear.

Dan. 10.9—falling—**E**—the preceding verse is very important: 'So I was left alone and saw this great vision, and no strength was left in me; my radiant appearance was fearfully changed, and I retained no strength'. This verse makes it seem likely that the falling over and sleeping is a natural reaction to the overwhelming character of the vision. That seems very different from the reports of those who fall over in the 'Toronto Blessing', the majority of whom do not have a vision or anything like it preceding their falling.

Hos. 11.10—roaring like a lion—**B F**.

Joel 2.12—weeping—**C E**—Joel invites the people of God to return to God 'with fasting, weeping and mourning'.

The context indicates weeping of repentance after a time of sinful living. It again does not apply to involuntary, ecstatic crying.

Amos 3.8—roaring—**B F**.

Mic. 1.8—strange noises, e.g. barking—**A E**—this verse describes Micah's expression of mourning over the fate of Judah which is declared in vv. 9-16. While modern Western people mourn in a very subdued manner, mourners in Old Testament times gave full expression to their grief, in terms both of their dress and their loud wailing. Here in v. 8 such actions and noises are described by means of animal metaphors. Most importantly, the verse very definitely describes mourning, and not the noises which result from some ecstatic experiences.

Hab. 3.16—trembling—**A**—see note on Ps. 2.11.

Mt. 17.6—falling—**E** (and probably **C**)—see note on Ezek. 1.28. Again, it is difficult to be sure whether this falling is voluntary or not, but it is worth noting that the Greek word for 'falling down' here (*epesan*) is the same as in Mt. 2.11, where the kings deliberately 'fall down' ('bow down' in NIV) and worship the baby Jesus. It is also the same word as in Mt. 18.26, 29 where the servants deliberately fall down to beg mercy from their masters. Notice also that in Mt.17.7 Jesus tells the disciples not to be afraid and to get up. He does not, for example, advise them to remain down on the ground so that they can receive more from the Spirit.

Mt. 28.4—trembling (and falling)—**E**—these are not the people of God. They are full of fear at what they see. They seem like frightened rabbits caught in the headlamp beams of a car.

Jn 17.13—laughter—**E**—certainly Jesus promises joy for his people, but there is no indication that it is ecstatic laughter.

Jn 18.6—falling—**E**—in light of the words, 'they drew back and fell to the ground', the best interpretation of this verse, it seems to me, is that the enemies of Jesus suddenly became afraid and threw themselves to the ground in order to express Jesus' supremacy over them. English translations say 'fell' not 'threw themselves', but the Greek word can mean both things. It is the same word as in Mt. 17.6.

Acts 2.13—drunkenness—**E**—this text commonly quoted in support of the 'Toronto Blessing'. However, as one supporter admits, 'That the 120 newly filled believers were acting in a "drunken" manner is what is known as an argument from silence.'[3] Proponents believe that though the text does not say the disciples were behaving drunkenly, this can be reasonably inferred from the words of the 'mockers'. I disagree very strongly.

The text says that some were 'mocking'. In the process of mocking, one person knowingly ridicules another. This may well include false accusations. Therefore, the mockers' words cannot be used to discover what was really happening. All we do know about what was happening is that, miraculously, by the power of the Holy Spirit, the believers were telling of the 'mighty works of God' in the hearers' own languages.

However, a little more can be said. In the 'Toronto Blessing' the majority of the phenomena do not make people appear drunk: jerking, shaking, 'pogoing' and roaring like lions are not things that are immediately associated with drunkenness. If Peter and the others had been doing these things, it seems far more likely that onlookers would have thought they were mad or even demon-possessed, not that they were drunk. Moreover, it is clear that they were not falling over and 'resting in the Lord' (to use a popular phrase), or lying on the floor kicking their legs in the air (a common 'Blessing' phenomenon), nor were they overcome with laughter. We know these things were not happening because the passage tells us they were standing, declaring the mighty works of God in foreign languages. This picture of them standing, declaring the mighty works of God, seems to me to be virtually incompatible with the idea that they were reeling about with loss of co-ordination of their limbs and speech in the 'drunken' manner displayed in the 'Blessing'.

In fact, the accusation of drunkenness is perfectly well explained by the fact that the disciples were standing in a group speaking all at one time in many different languages not their own. To some of the onlookers this may have seemed like meaningless babble, much like a group of drunks would make when they have lost control of their speech. In my view, therefore, the only phenomenon which the reference to drunkenness need have behind it is the 'speaking in tongues' which the text has already told us about.

Acts 4.31—shaking—**B**—the building is shaken, not the people.

Acts 9.4—falling—**E**—once again, it is impossible to be completely sure whether this falling is voluntary or not, but it seems to me the best interpretation is that Paul (who is still an enemy of Jesus at this point) throws himself to the ground in fear, on experiencing a terrible vision. See notes on Jn 18.6 and Mt. 17.6.

Acts 10.10—falling—**E**—Peter falls into a trance in which he receives a vision, he does not fall over.

Rom. 8.22-23—groaning—**A F**—the verses tell us this groaning is metaphorical: creation is unable literally to 'groan' and the text says Christians 'groan inwardly', not out loud.

1 Cor. 2.3—trembling—**A**—the phrase 'in fear and trembling' (*en phobo kai en tromo*) seems to be a stock phrase (it also occurs in 2 Cor. 7.15, Eph. 6.5 and Phil. 2.2) used by Paul to refer to a right attitude of humility and reverence towards others. This is perhaps made most clear by Eph. 6.5: 'Slaves, be obedient to those who are your earthly masters, with fear and trembling, in singleness of heart, as to Christ'. In 1 Cor. 2.3 the phrase is used by Paul to describe his attitude of service and humility towards his fellow Christians (or perhaps towards God, or perhaps both) throughout the time he was with the Corinthian church. It is not a physical description. See also note on Phil. 2.12.

2 Cor. 5.4—groaning—**A**—see note on Rom 8.22-23.

2 Cor. 12.1-4—falling—**E**—Paul speaks of an amazing experience, but does not mention falling over.

Phil. 2.12—trembling—**A**—here, Paul is not telling the Philippians to start having Toronto-type experiences. 'Work out your salvation with fear and trembling' means 'live lives of humility, love and unity, following the example of Christ, and do this with an attitude which can metaphorically be described as "fear and trembling"'. The context of the verse confirms this. The verse begins with the word 'therefore', and refers us back to vv. 5-11, in which Paul describes Christ's attitude of self-sacrifice and service toward his fellow human beings, and to vv. 1-4, in which Paul tells the Philippians to love and serve each other. Verse 12 is a summary of what Paul expects them to conclude from vv. 1-11. See also note on 1 Cor. 2.3.

Eph. 5.18—drunkenness—**E**—some supporters of the 'Blessing' think there is a physical similarity between being 'drunk with wine' and 'being filled with the Spirit'. However, the verse does not tell us that, but seems instead to offer a strong contrast between drunkenness and the Spirit-filled life. The following verses explain what the outward appearance of 'being filled with the Spirit' is: 'be filled with the Spirit, addressing one another in psalms and hymns and spiritual songs, singing and making melody to the Lord with all your heart, always and for everything giving thanks in the name of our Lord Jesus Christ to God the Father' (Eph. 5.18b-20). This is far from reeling about in a drunken manner. The 'ordinary' Spirit-filled life will give us fulfilment and joy, and so is far better than a life of drunkenness.

James 2.19—trembling—**B**.

Rev. 1.17—falling—**E** (perhaps **C**)—see note on Jn 18.6. (The phrase 'fell at his feet as though dead' need only imply that John, on seeing the fearful vision, lay absolutely still, like a frightened animal feigning death.)

Rev. 5.5—roaring like a lion—**B E F**.

Rev. 10.3—roaring like a lion—**B F**.

The conclusion from assessing all these texts is that none of them are sufficient to endorse 'Toronto Blessing' type physical phenomena as biblical. In various different ways, they each fail to fulfil the criteria that would enable someone to say that what we are seeing is approved by the Bible.

We need to be very clear about what I am saying here. First, I am certainly not saying that it is unbiblical to laugh or cry, for example, in church services. I would thoroughly endorse such expressions of emotion as a legitimate part of Christian gatherings. However, the issue with the 'Toronto Blessing' is not 'normal' but ecstatic laughter and tears—laughter and tears induced in altered states of consciousness. There is no biblical text which can be shown to endorse such laughing and crying. No doubt there have also been many occasions in 'Blessing' meetings on which people have laughed 'normally' and cried 'normally', but it is the ecstatic phenomena which are the issue.

Second, I am not saying that 'strange' things do not happen in the Bible. 'Strange' things do happen to some biblical figures, and there is no reason to think that they cannot happen to people now. But the key point is that typical 'Blessing' experiences are significantly different from the experiences had by the biblical figures. They are so different that it is impossible to maintain that, for example, typical 'Blessing'-type falling is the same as that found in the Bible. This is not to say that no falling experience had by those involved in the 'Blessing' is similar to the biblical ones—I cannot know the content of every experience. But it is to say that typical 'Blessing' falling experiences are significantly different. The same is true of the typical shaking and trembling phenomena.

Third, I am prepared to go further with regard to the drunkenness phenomenon. Those who assert that biblical figures displayed this phenomenon are basing their claim on an extremely flimsy argument from silence, which in turn is based on the words of some anti-Christian mockers. My comments above on Acts 2.13 make it clear why we should not accept the argument. The only 'drunkenness' spoken of in the Bible is that induced by alcohol, and it is something of which the Bible disapproves. The claim that 'Toronto Blessing' 'drunkenness' is the divine alternative to alcoholic drunkenness is, of course, just as flimsy an argument from silence. See my comments on Eph. 5.18 for why it should be rejected.

Fourth, there are appropriate occasions for people to roar and make other strange noises. There is no reason why somebody should not roar like a lion in a play, for example; and it might be appropriate to do so within a Christian service. It might even be appropriate for somebody to roar like a lion as part of their delivery of a prophetic message. However, this is not what is happening in typical 'Blessing' experiences. In the latter, the noises are uttered as part of an ecstatic experience, not as part of a prophetic message. To claim that the noises 'are prophetic' or 'accompany the prophetic'[4] does not answer this objection. Calling a thing 'prophetic' does not actually make it prophetic. The simple fact of the matter is that there is no biblical precedent for people ecstatically uttering strange animal noises while under the influence of the Holy Spirit. As John Stott says, 'The whole Bible tells us that we are different from the animal creation; it rebukes us when we behave like animals and calls us to be distinct. Nebuchadnezzar's animal behaviour was under the judgement, not the blessing, of God.'[5]

Finally, this Appendix explains why I believe we must reject the claim that the typical physical phenomena of the 'Toronto Blessing' are 'in the Bible'. It does not do more than that. It does not, for example, prove that they are wrong, though I think it does point in that direction for at least some of them. However, the fact that the 'Blessing' phenomena are not in the Bible is very significant. It means that the simplest way of demonstrating them to be 'biblical' is not available to supporters of the 'Blessing'. If such supporters wish to be faithful to the authority of the Bible, therefore, they will need to do some hard and fast work at demonstrating the 'Blessing' to be 'biblical' in some other way. Elsewhere in this book I have demonstrated why those 'other ways' which have been attempted so far have also failed.

NOTES

1. This is quoted in M. Stibbe, *Times of Refreshing* (London: Marshall Pickering, 1995), p. 108.
2. B. Jackson, 'What in the World is Happening to Us? A Biblical Perspective on Renewal' (a paper circulated by Toronto Airport Vineyard), p. 5.
3. Ibid, p. 6.
4. See, for example, D. Pytches, 'The Blessings and the Concerns' in *Renewal* magazine (December, 1994, No. 223), p. 15.
5. See 'Life in the Spirit of Truth' in *Third Way* magazine (October 1995, 18.8), p. 22.

APPENDIX 2

Individuals' Experiences

Proponents of the 'Toronto Blessing' make individuals' experiences and their testimonies about them the linchpin of their arguments. I have shown that this is a mistake. The belief that the 'Blessing' is a movement initiated and sustained by God revolves around this false application of the 'fruit' argument. Nevertheless, outside of the arena of polemics, it is important that individuals have a way of assessing and evaluating their own experiences. In this Appendix I want offer what I hope is a helpful way of doing that. The approach I will take is to offer three categories of experience, the 'good', the 'bad' and the 'indifferent', and describe what I think are the defining features of each.

The Good

I have argued that the 'Toronto Blessing' is best understood as a movement of subconscious exploration. It is not, therefore, what those who are involved have thought it to be. But I have also argued that this does not automatically mean every experience which those involved have had is bad. There is room to say that some experiences can have been good.

We can be a little more precise about this if we make a distinction between what I will call 'natural good' and 'spiritual good'. Both types of good come from God, the former insofar as human beings receive good things through God's good creation, the latter insofar as human beings receive good things more directly through the Holy Spirit.

This is a useful distinction (though it should not be pushed too far).

'Natural Good'

Christians engage in a lot of things which do them good and which non-christians also engage in. Many people play sports, for example, and it does them good, both physically and mentally. Sport is something through which we can receive 'natural good'. Sport is a non-religious activity, but even religious activities have elements to them which do us 'natural good'. For example, whatever else it does, singing worship songs is 'naturally good' for us because singing in general does us good. Singing is an enjoyable activity (at least for most people), and it helps us relieve stress and be mentally refreshed. This is not all worship singing does, but it is part of it.

In my view, there is no doubt that 'Blessing' experiences also do some 'natural good' for some people. Some people have found their experience to be enjoyable. In a small way, that does good. For some, it has been more than that. They have found great emotional and mental relief through being able to disengage their consciousness to some extent and allow their subconscious to express itself, perhaps—in some cases—to release considerable hidden pain or tension. It seems likely to me that times of ecstatic laughter or weeping can do good in this way. They can have good therapeutic effects. I think that this is what the trained psychotherapist was getting at who is reported as saying to a church leader,

> that she and her colleagues would 'give their right arm' to see in their surgeries what was happening in his church building. She added, 'It takes us two or

211

three years to get people to this point.' She could see it was happening in 20-30 minutes and sometimes even two or three minutes! She concluded that this is very healthy.[1]

We will see in the section entitled 'the bad', that there are reasons for not being quite so optimistic, but I think it is fair to say that for some people it has been healthy. It has given them some healthy experiences. But we need to note that healthy experiences can, by definition, only bring short-term improvements. Health must be maintained. If an unhealthy person went to a health farm, for instance, when they went back to their normal environment they would be likely to quickly become unhealthy again unless they changed their circumstances.

We also have to say that 'healthy experiences' cannot provide justification for making 'Blessing' meetings part of church services. Making them part of church services implies that what is going on is 'spiritually good', not just 'naturally good'. It implies that this is a specifically Christian activity, with specifically Christian content. When we sing in church, we sing songs with a particular Christian content, and so make our singing 'worship'. If it did not have that content, it would still be healthy but it would be wrong to make it part of church services or to call it 'worship'.

Finally, there is the possibility that an experience can bring good changes at the subconscious level. It does seem some people after their experience are left feeling more confident and at ease with the world. Sometimes, these changes seem to be permanent. It may be that this is simply because they perceive their experience to be 'proof' that God loves them personally, which they had doubted before, and so their view of their place in the world changes. Or it may be that a change takes place at the subconscious level in some other way which we do not understand. For example, Mick Brown describes the changes that were wrought in one woman by her experience at the hands of the Hindu avatar he also visited as follows:

> I've spoken to other people who have taken darshan with Mother Meera, several of whom said that their lives had changed in quite fundamental ways as a result. One woman a French university lecturer, who had been two or three times to the darshan, had noticed that at first very slightly, but then un-mistakably, this change had come over her. Whereas previously she had been rather insular, and was not someone that people would necessarily turn to, as a result of those experiences she gradually began to feel in herself a sense that she was more expansive to the world, and suddenly, without any reason, people started to turn to her more for advice, to lean on her. It was as if the more strength she had in herself, the more she could draw on this reservoir of strength she felt she had found.[2]

It sounds to me like these consequences were due to a significant change for the good in her subconscious, effected by the avatar. It seems possible that the 'Toronto Blessing' also causes such changes in some people.

'Spiritual Good'

I defined 'spiritual good' as something which comes 'more directly through the Holy Spirit'. A very great number of people believe themselves to have received something good in this sense through the 'Toronto Blessing'. Now, I explained in Chapter 9 that, because God is gracious and patient, it is indeed possible for someone to have received something from the Holy Spirit in and through the 'Blessing'. However, we need to be very tough-minded and say that the majority of those who believe themselves to have received 'spiritual good' are mistaken.

We need to be tough-minded, because if we are not then the work of the Holy Spirit will be enormously devalued. Christians must be prepared to admit they were mistaken, that they had a strange experience and over-interpreted it as a work of God. As I noted in Chapter 8, that is something charismatics in particular are prone to do, though it is something Christians in general and indeed all human beings are prone to do to some extent. Throughout history countless 'strange things' have happened but, relatively speaking, only a few of them are due to the direct activity of God. If we are not clear about this, then we will be unable to distinguish those occasions.

Paradoxically, charismatics' great desire to see God at work is in danger of preventing us from proclaiming his work among us with any credibility. A good example of this is found in the area of physical healing. In recent years there has been a proliferation of 'miraculous healing ministries' in Britain. These have tended to claim great results and, out of their desire to see God at work, ordinary charismatics have gone along with it. The plain fact of the matter is that, when investigated, very few of the supposed healings turn out to be what is claimed. Many healing ministries play on the fact that when they hold meetings, the charismatics who make up the vast majority of the audience want to see things happen and will interpret strange sensations in their bodies as 'healing'. Thus, to those who are there at the time, the meetings appear to get results. But checks are very rarely made afterwards to see whether anything long-term happened, and when checks are made, the claimed healings tend to dissolve away into nothing. But that does not matter, since during the meetings people appear to have been healed, and it is this which makes the ministry successful.

The rest of Britain is well aware of this state of affairs. The TV and the Press occasionally investigate claims of miraculous healings, and find them to be wanting. So charismatics tend to lose credibility, and our claims that God is at work among us are not believed. As a result, when God does actually heal people it has virtually no impact at all. This is an area in which we have failed to be tough-minded and have paid a heavy price.

The 'Toronto Blessing' is an area in which we are failing in a similar way. I am thinking not so much of physical healing (though quite a number of unsubstantiated claims about healings have been made, to add to the early excitement), but of the claims to have 'heard from God'. It is crucial that people begin to be honest and admit it to themselves when they have over-interpreted their experiences. The kind of thing I mean is when a person who experiences ecstatic laughter interprets it as God telling him that he is laughing with joy over him. Another person experiences ecstatic laughter and she interprets it as God telling her he laughs in derision at the rebellion of the nations. Another person might experience ecstatic weeping, and interpret it as God telling him he is weeping with him over the hurt he feels from his past. Yet another might experience ecstatic weeping, and interpret it as God telling her he weeps over the lost people of the world.

These things do express truths: God is joyful about his children, he does hold rebellion against him in derision, and so on. And, in a sense, these peoples' experiences have been valuable. But I believe it is often not the case that God has told them these things, but that their ecstatic experience has reminded them of a truth which they already know. The experience may be extremely valuable, because it causes the person to grasp hold of the truth much more confidently than before and believe it in a much more wholehearted sense. But it is not accurate to claim that they heard from God. This distinction may seem merely academic, but I believe it is very important. To claim to have been reminded of and have grasped a spiritual truth is one thing, to claim to have heard from God is another.

Having said all that, it is still possible that some people have indeed heard from God during an experience. God is a good, loving God who does speak to his people. And he is free to do so whenever and however he wishes. He is also free and able to bring repentance, healing and many other good things to whomever he wants. Therefore, I see no reason to think that some people cannot have received 'spiritual good'. But I must repeat: this does not mean the 'Toronto Blessing' as a movement is 'of God'.

The Bad

There have been some people whose experiences have been bad for them. Supporters of the 'Blessing' should take this much more seriously than they have done so far. While perhaps the majority have either felt some benefit from their experience or have found it indifferent, there are others who have felt damaged and confused. There are a number of ways this may have happened.

First, we need to consider the down side of seeing the 'Toronto Blessing' as therapeutic. I mentioned earlier the report of a trained psychotherapist which stated that she and her colleagues would 'give their right arm' to see in their surgeries what was happening in the 'Blessing'. I consider her next words to be very significant. She said, 'It takes us two or three years to get people to this point.'[3]

Presumably, people who undergo psychotherapy have some fairly serious mental disorders. During those 'two or three years', their problems can be assessed and suitable treatment decided on. They and the therapist can carefully think through what would be helpful and what would be damaging for them. The right time for treatment and for emotional release can be carefully chosen. And of course, there is on-going aftercare beyond the treatment.

With the 'Blessing' none of this happens. People reach emotional catharsis in a matter of minutes. That probably does not matter for those who are mentally healthy, but it is foolish in the extreme to assume it will always be good for people who are suffering some sort of mental disorder. It will be just as likely to do them harm. The only thing that could definitely protect them against this would be if it truly was the Holy Spirit who was bringing about the catharsis. And this is what people involved are assuming. But we have already seen reason to doubt it.

Like other people, Christians suffer from depression. For some, this is so serious as to be called 'clinical depression', while for others it is a milder form of the condition. It seems likely to me that, even for those who suffer mild depression, the 'Blessing' is likely to have done damage. This is because many of them will reach a 'high' during their experience without having the underlying reasons for their depression dealt with. Such 'highs' will only magnify the unsatisfactory nature of their ordinary lives as they see them. That is especially true for people who are encouraged to 'testify' soon after their experience. Once they have testified, it is not just them but also their hearers who believe that God has done a great work in them. When the individual comes to realise that this is not the case, he or she will have not just his or her own disappointment to deal with, but also the guilt of having misled the hearers and the weight of their disappointment. Consequently, they may well become more depressed. The consequences for those who are clinically depressed or suffer some other sort of mental disorder may be far worse.

Second, if, as I outlined earlier, for reasons we cannot understand the 'Toronto Blessing' causes relatively long-lasting changes for the good at the subconscious level in some people, then it may similarly cause changes for the worse in others. I know at least one person to whom this seems to have happened. She has been left feeling 'spiritually disturbed' by what happened to her.

Third, for some people, their experiences have had the bad effect of leaving them confused. This happens because, as I argued in Chapter 8, the experiences are essentially 'spiritually neutral' experiences to which those involved have to give their own interpretation. The majority of people give them the interpretation offered by the leaders of the movement, that they are experiences inspired by the Holy Spirit, but some feel unable to accept this. For many different reasons, the dominant interpretation does not work for them. Perhaps the commonest reason is that the experience felt bad and frightening and so they are unable to believe that God 'did it to them'. They are left in a state of confusion as to what it was that really happened.

Finally, there are those who, despite badly wanting an experience, have, for whatever reason, not 'received' one. Many of these people feel rejected by God and inferior to those who have 'received'. Some churches have provided teaching and counselling to help them deal with these feelings. But, unfortunately, for some people, psychologically speaking, that is not enough. Feelings of rejection and inferiority can remain despite even the strongest affirmations that 'God loves everybody'.

It is to be hoped that, whether or not the leaders of churches involved in the 'Toronto Blessing' agree with the argument of this book, they will at least begin to take these bad effects more seriously. I believe they have a pastoral duty to all who have 'Blessing' experiences, not just to those who find their experiences to be good. Church leaders need to begin to make room for people who have had bad experiences to speak about them without being stigmatised as 'demonised' or 'against God'. Bad experiences are just as much a part of the 'Toronto Blessing' as the good experiences are. Leaders must not add to the bad by allowing people who have had bad experiences to be marginalised and isolated. At present, there is a real danger of this happening.

The Indifferent

There are a great many people for whom 'Toronto Blessing' experiences have been indifferent. I want to include in this category two main types. First, there are a lot of people who have had something happen to them, but who have found nothing spiritually significant in their experience. It might have felt unusual, perhaps quite nice, perhaps a little uncomfortable, but essentially it was an empty experience. Second, there are a lot of people who have made themselves available in meetings (perhaps repeatedly) to 'receive' something, but have felt nothing.

Empty Experience

If people are honest with themselves and each other, they will realise that a great deal of their experiences come into this category. For many people who have displayed the strange phenomena of the 'Blessing', their experience has made no difference at all. In the light of what I have said elsewhere in this book, this is not surprising. Essentially, the experiences are composed of altered states of consciousness and their physical effects. For many people, there is nothing more to them than that.

There really is little more to be said under this category, other than to encourage those who have had only 'empty experiences' to put them behind them and get back to the mainstream of 'normal' Christianity. Charismatic Christians must stop belittling ordinary life and realise that the Holy Spirit is interested much more in the ordinary than in the extraordinary. He wants to help us make Jesus Lord in everyday life, in work, leisure, families and friendships. Being a Christian is not about displaying amazing manifestations of power. It is about leading a life which bears witness to Jesus Christ. Charismatic Christians ought to be concerned with the power of love, not the love of power. As Christians, we have the wonderful hope of the resurrection victory set before us, but it is to a life of self-giving love and service, a life represented by the crucifixion, that we have been called.

No Experience

There are many people involved in the 'Toronto Blessing' who have never actually experienced the phenomena for themselves. I have already mentioned people for whom the lack of experience leads to feelings of rejection and inferiority. There are others who are actually relieved that they have not had to display the rather embarrassing phenomena they see in others. For others again, their lack of experiences has been a matter of indifference. However, among both those who feel relieved and those who feel indifferent there are many who continue to support the 'Blessing'. Indeed, the number of church leaders who have had few or no experiences themselves, yet who support the 'Blessing', is surprisingly high. Some of its most vociferous supporters come into this category. My guess is that this is because they are people who, naturally and by training as leaders, tend to keep control of situations, and who therefore do not easily disengage their consciousness. There are, of course, other factors, but I suspect that this is an important one.

Whatever the reasons, there are people who have not had 'Blessing' experiences. There is little more to be said about this, other than what I said a moment ago about the need to get back to the mainstream of 'normal' Christianity. People who have not had experiences themselves have nevertheless been part of (and sometimes even orchestrators of) a period of time in which much 'normal' church life has been abandoned. They need to encourage their churches to put aside the distraction of the 'Toronto Blessing' and get on with the mission to which God has called his people: to reach and serve a world which desperately needs the life God offers through the body of Christ.

NOTES
1. See G. Coates, '"Toronto" and Scripture', in *Renewal* magazine (November, 1994.,No. 222), p. 27.
2. This appears in 'What Happened Next?', in *Evangelicals Now* newspaper (February, 1995), p. 8.
3. See G. Coates, '"Toronto" and Scripture', p. 27.